70 Seasonal Drinks
Infused with Magic & Ritual

WitchCraft Cocktails

Julia Halina Hadas

Adams Media

New York • London • Toronto • Sydney • New Delhi

A **adams**media

Adams Media
An Imprint of Simon & Schuster, Inc.
100 Technology Center Drive
Stoughton, MA 02072

First Adams Media hardcover edition September 2020

ADAMS MEDIA and colophon are trademarks of Simon & Schuster.

For information about special discounts for bulk purchases, please contact Simon & Schuster Special Sales at 1-866-506-1949 or business@simonandschuster.com.

The Simon & Schuster Speakers Bureau can bring authors to your live event. For more information or to book an event contact the Simon & Schuster Speakers Bureau at 1-866-248-3049 or visit our website at www.simonspeakers.com.

Interior design by Sylvia McArdle
Interior photographs by Harper Point Photography; all other interior images © 123RF;
The Golden Thread Tarot card images that were employed in the photographs throughout this book are under the copyright of Tina Gong copyright © 2016 and used with permission. All rights reserved.

Printed in the United States of America

5 2021

Library of Congress Cataloging-in-Publication Data
Names: Hadas, Julia Halina, author.
Title: WitchCraft cocktails / Julia Halina Hadas.
Description: Avon, Massachusetts: Adams Media, 2020. | Includes bibliographical references and index.
Identifiers: LCCN 2020011315 | ISBN 9781507213933 (hc) | ISBN 9781507213940 (ebook)
Subjects: LCSH: Witchcraft. | Formulas, recipes, etc. | Food--Miscellanea. | Cocktails. | Magic.
Classification: LCC BF1572.R4 H33 2020 | DDC 133.4/3--dc23
LC record available at https://lccn.loc.gov/2020011315

ISBN 978-1-5072-1393-3
ISBN 978-1-5072-1394-0 (ebook)

Always follow safety and commonsense cooking protocols while using kitchen utensils, operating ovens and stoves, and handling uncooked food. If children are assisting in the preparation of any recipe, they should always be supervised by an adult.

Dedication

To the numerous family members, friends, coworkers, and spirits
who supported me in this endeavor. Special thanks to my mother
and Rolf, as well as Eileen, Sarah, and all of Adams Media for the
opportunity and continuous support.

Contents

Introduction

Like many modern witchcraft practices, the celebration of magic and ritual with infused potables extends deep into human history. Open the cover of any introductory witchcraft book, and you'll find steps to extract the essence of rose to create a magical water for beauty, or advice on what type of wine is best to leave as an offering for a deity. A witch might use alcohol to create tinctures to manifest good communication with loved ones, or aromatic mists to balance a chakra that has been blocked. And what's a coven gathering without a seasonal libation?

In *WitchCraft Cocktails*, these practices are given new life and a modern twist. In Part I, you'll learn how to imbue herbs, crystals, and other instruments of the ethereal realm with different alcohols and syrups for delicious drinks that heighten your spells—or work as complete spells. Organized by season, the recipes in Part 2 draw power from astrological signs, planets, crystals, tarot cards, and special events linked to fall, winter, spring, and summer.

Entice love and boldness with a Venus Spritzer, draw insights from philosophical Sagittarius with The Jasmine Archer, invite creativity with a carnelian-infused Mocha Persuasion, and more.

You'll also delve deeper into the invaluable relationship between witchcraft and cocktails, as well as the magical properties of different spirits and how to blend them like a seasoned mixologist. Devote some time to exploring these initial pages before crafting your own potions, so you can unlock the full potential of each recipe. Whether you are anointing a candle for financial prosperity or imbibing the energies of the moon for inner growth and transformation, there's a corresponding cocktail to elevate your magical work.

PART 1
The World of Witchcraft & Alcohol

CHAPTER 1

Alcohol & Witchcraft Intertwined

Thousands of years ago, Sumerian women monitored the fermentation of beer by singing the *Hymn to Ninkasi* (the Sumerian brewing goddess), for a successful yield. Today, a seasoned mixologist blends carefully chosen spirits and syrups for a delicious concoction that somehow evokes creativity in the recipient. While alcohol and spiritual practices may seem radically different and separate at first, their entwined history tells another story—one that unlocks the potential for even more magic moving forward.

In this chapter, you will unravel the thread of alcohol's woven history within witchcraft to uncover the modern cocktail's beginnings as a spiritual offering, how it's used in magic today, and how it can be used in the future of witchcraft. It's time for your journey into witchcraft cocktails to begin!

THE HISTORIC ROOTS OF ALCOHOL IN WITCHCRAFT

Alcohol's ability to preserve the energetic essence and flavor of herbs makes it essential in any witch's cabinet, and its relaxing and anesthetizing effects gave it prominence in early healing practices. As far back as ancient Rome, wine was cooked with different spices and herbs to help protect against seasonal cold and illnesses. The ancient Chinese used alcohol blends to help balance stomach maladies and inspire good moods and strength. And in ancient Egypt, beer was a source of nourishment and clean water during long days working out in the heat.

Across the ancient world, alcohol was also a tool for ceremony and reverence of the gods. In what is now Henan Province in China, pottery jars were used to ferment wine made from rice, honey, and various fruits for religious rituals surrounding the dead. In the burial chambers of Enheduanna, the Sumerian priestess of the moon god Nanna, sacred drinking tools were discovered showing the spiritual connection of alcohol as a way to commune with the gods.

WITCHCRAFT AND ALCOHOL TODAY

Alcohol is the physical manifestation of the fruits of the harvest season and the earth's bounty, and is still very much a part of witchcraft and religion today. Various modern cultural and witchcraft practices continue to use spirits as an offering: In Christianity, wine represents the blood of Christ and is sipped during Communion; in Afro-Caribbean practices, rum is poured for protection and as an offering to different spirits and deities; in ancestral worship, a witch pours a liquor pertaining to their ancestral roots in an offering cup.

Brewing in itself is a magical act. All four elements come into play through the combination of heat (fire); moisture (water); herbs and grains (earth); and the gusts of air that introduce natural alcohol-producing yeasts, or the resulting intoxicating herbal steam and evaporation of pure alcohol. With every alcoholic beverage, the elements have been combined and utilized to create something utterly different and transformative.

Strengthening the Connection

The growing popularity of aromatic healing mists, crystal elixirs, and flower essences complement alcohol's ability to infuse, preserve, and hold the energy of various herbs and other ingredients. These energies are also known in the witchcraft world as "vibrations," referring to the idea that everything on earth contains an invisible energy that radiates from it. Witches harness these energies as part of their magical work.

However, there is so much more that can be done within the relationship between witchcraft and alcohol—so much magical potential waiting to be unlocked! As Scott Cunningham lays out in his book *Cunningham's Encyclopedia of Wicca in the Kitchen*, ingesting food, fruit, and herbs with resonating correspondences can elevate magical endeavors. For example, if a witch wants to inspire love, they may eat papaya glazed with honey as they burn a pink candle. But you can go a level deeper by incorporating those flavors in alcohol. Create a powerful cocktail with oh-so-delicious Hibiscus-Rose Honey Syrup, and sip away to invite that love into a current or future relationship.

Beyond enhancing a spell, the magic of cocktails can be used in your witchcraft to inspire the specific energy needed to produce a potent spell in the first place. After all, one key part of witchcraft is visualization—imagining what it would look and feel like to have a desired outcome. For instance, think about a confidence spell to get the attention of someone you like, or to help you speak up at work. What would that confidence look like? What would it feel like? If you try to do a confidence spell without any preparation, it can be a challenge to muster up that visualization and truly believe in it. And if you don't believe that outcome is possible, you will sabotage your spell. Enjoying a correctly aligned herbal cocktail beforehand can help you manifest the confident energy you need to believe in your spell.

As you continue through the following chapters, you will uncover more and more of the mystical powers found in combining witchcraft with alcohol.

ENCHANTED LIBATIONS AND RESPONSIBILITY

Magical infusions are a wonderful way to propel your magic to the next level, but it is important to enjoy them responsibly. Not only will you be caring for your well-being, but you will also set yourself up for effective spellwork. Even the Cult of Dionysus and ancient Sumerians promoted the use of alcohol in moderation! You can also make any cocktail alcohol-free—but still full of magic—by replacing the alcohol with soda water. You'll likely want to add more soda water, and also adjust the sugar-to-citrus ratios per your preference. If it is a shaken cocktail, add the soda water after shaking, or else you'll have an explosion.

It is also important to consider the proper use of different herbs before use. There are plenty of resources online that provide more information and safety instructions, and you can talk to your doctor about their recommendations as well.

TURNING THE PAGE

With a more comprehensive understanding of how witchcraft and alcohol are intertwined, you are ready to dive into the basics of bartending, from what materials you will need to the unique connections of different alcohols to the magical realm. As countless witches from the past have understood, there is much more to alcohol than simple good taste.

Bartending Basics

Witchcraft is about tapping into the energetic web of the universe, the seasonal changes and offerings, and owning your own divinity and power, to produce a desired outcome. So every part of the process needs to be handled with care, which means understanding which alcohol is best for a given situation and how to use the different tools and techniques involved in mixing up the perfect cocktail.

In this chapter, you will discover a simple guide to bartending, from the difference between vodka and gin to what exactly a muddler is and how to use it. Regardless of whether you are new to mixing drinks or have a few tricks up your sleeve already, you will find everything you need to create eye-catching libations like a seasoned bartender.

ALCOHOL VARIETALS

Ancient alchemists developed the pot still (a closed chamber where a fermented substance is added and then heated to separate alcohol from other matter) to distill the alcoholic spirits of various plants. Depending on the plant used, a different type of alcohol would result from this process, such as gin or tequila. And just as herbs and flowers have varying energies and magical associations, so does each type of alcohol. These unique qualities indicate what kinds of spells and rituals each alcohol type is best used in. Because these alcohols will form the base of your magical cocktails, it is important to understand the enchanted potential tied to each.

Absinthe

Once incorrectly described as a hallucinogen, striking green absinthe is also known as the "Green Fairy." Modern absinthe is made using a long list of botanicals, including green anise, Florence fennel, and wormwood. It has a strong anise flavor.

Due to wormwood's associations with psychic ability and contacting spirits, it is a go-to in magic surrounding connecting to fairies and also for psychic work. Bewitching, often mysterious absinthe is the perfect aid in bridging the gap between the physical and ethereal realms.

Beer

Beer is made from the mash and fermentation of various grains, usually barley, corn, and hops. It is believed to be the oldest type of alcohol intentionally created, and historians note that women were responsible for brewing beer in ancient societies. The type of beer depends on which grains and yeasts are used to brew it.

With its grain base, beer is a natural choice for celebrating the summer and fall harvests, and commemorating those harvests in the cold of winter. Its carbonation makes it a perfect cocktail topper as well. According to *Cunningham's Encyclopedia of Wicca in the Kitchen*, beer is excellent for purification work. In fact, there are even spas that offer a soak in a tub of beer!

Wine

Wine has been revered and used for deity worship for centuries. Unlike beer, however, wine is most commonly made from the fermentation of grapes (though it can be made from other fruits). Depending on when the skins of the grapes are removed, a different type of wine—red, white, or rosé—will result from this fermentation. To make red wine, the skins are left on throughout the process; for white wine, the skins are removed in the earlier stages; and for rosé, the skins are left on for a shorter period of time than red and for longer than white.

Due to the nature of its creation with the grape skins, red wine is associated with the physical body, vitality, energy, and ancestors. White wine energies are more spiritual and soul-aligned in nature. Rosé, with its pink hue, is often associated with love. Seen as "in between" red and white wine, it can also represent a connection between the physical and spiritual.

Brandy

Brandy is a liquor distilled from wine. It usually contains less alcohol than whiskey or vodka. As a product of grape distillation, brandy is a potent alcohol for spiritual offerings, and depending on the type of brandy (such as apple brandy for love and fertility), it can be used for a number of specific magic workings.

Vodka

Vodka is a clear, distilled beverage made from the fermentation of any organic substance. While it is commonly made from grain or potatoes, that is not a requirement in the United States. Vodka is usually distilled to a high proof, such as 180 proof (90 percent alcohol), to which water is later added before it is sold. Because it is brought to such a high alcohol percentage and not flavored with anything other than the faint leftover flavors of its base ingredients, vodka is the most neutral of the distilled spirits. This neutrality makes vodka the most popular choice for mists and tinctures, as it preserves and enhances the energies of the herbs used without adding much flavor or scent. This also makes vodka fantastic for clarity magic.

Gin

While vodka can be made from any organic substance, gin is defined solely by the addition and prominent flavor of juniper berries. At whatever point the juniper is added, as an infusion before or after distillation, it becomes gin. Often, distilleries will add various other herbal flavors to complement and bring out the unique flavors of this otherwise herbal medicinal beverage. Juniper's protective, cleansing associations make gin a go-to for cleansing, reversing, and protective cocktails.

Mezcal

Mezcal, which includes tequila, is distilled from the agave plant. The agave plant is a late bloomer—it blooms only once after ten to twenty-five years of growing and then quickly dies. Its unique life cycle and close relationship to the asparagus plant makes mezcal wonderful for rejuvenation, inspiring love, and magical workings around stepping into one's power. Tequila—made only from the blue agave plant—features a "cleaner" flavor profile, whereas mezcal, from the green agave plant, carries a smoky essence akin to Scotch whisky.

Both can be aged in wooden barrels for some time, allowing the alcohol to pull out flavor nuances from the wood. The amount of time the spirit has been aged is designated by the terms *silver*, *reposado*, and *anejo*.

Whiskey

Whiskey is made from a fermented grain mash. Grains such as barley, corn, rye, and wheat are usually used, and depending on the percentage of the herb, this can yield bourbons or rye whiskeys. After distillation, the alcohol is then aged in barrels (often charred oak barrels), where the alcohol soaks up flavor over time. With the influence of grains and oak, whiskey is another prominent alcohol for the harvest season, as well as for grounding, ancestral work, and prosperity.

Rum

Rum is made from the distillation of sugarcane juice or molasses, and it can also be aged to add different flavors. White rum is the filtered, water-cut version of what comes directly off the still. It is a popular, more neutral base in a variety of cocktails. Dark rum,

however, is usually aged in wooden barrels or combined with caramel or burnt sugar to give it a rich molasses flavor. Rum is used in many modern Afro-Caribbean traditions and as offerings to the deities of these traditions. Due to its sugarcane roots, rum is great in workings that involve winning someone's favor. Additionally, this aspect makes rum perfect for protection and neutralizing negative energy.

Liqueurs

Liqueurs are the result of adding sugar and various herbs and fruits to alcohols. These are typically used in conjunction with a stronger base alcohol, like vodka or whiskey. They are a perfect way to layer on and create nuanced flavors without adding too much sweetness. The most common liqueurs are orange liqueurs, such as triple sec, dry curaçao, and Grand Marnier.

Other Alcohols

The desire to take advantage of the healing benefits attributed to herbal alcohol infusions has resulted in many unique beverages. Italian herbal liqueurs, such as aperitifs and digestifs, were created to stimulate appetite and inspire better digestion. And some recipes, such as Chartreuse 1605 (created by monks in the Chartreuse Mountains of

France as a medicine following the discovery of a manuscript containing an elixir for long life), are made in secret.

It seems there are as many liqueurs and liquors as there are stars in the sky, and every day, new types are being created—each with its own unique flavors and magical possibilities. It is recommended that you first practice spellwork with the alcohols listed in this chapter before experimenting with other varieties.

ALCOHOL AND WATER

Under the light of the full moon, witches lay out pure water to be charged. Under sunlight, they charge crystals with this water to create crystal elixirs. Water is one of the most magical, life-inducing substances on earth, and also one of the most susceptible to vibration. Author Masaru Emoto spent his career studying the molecular change in water that occurs as a result of environment and human consciousness. More specifically, his research showed that the structure of water changes based on whether negative or positive words (or intentions) were spoken to it. These energies—or vibrations—made a tangible impact.

Water is often added to alcoholic beverage recipes (as ice). Because water carries energy, you will want to be selective in the water(s) you add to your own drinks. The type of water you use to make your ice matters too. Ice sitting in the freezer can have a stale energy and taste, affecting the quality and flavor of your magical cocktails. To charge your own water for ice or alcohol, place it in a closed Mason jar in the moonlight. You can also freeze a flower into an ice cube for floral vibrations and a lovely garnish.

THE TOOLS

When it comes to creating your own cocktails, there are certain tools you will want to use to control the flavors and their expression. Ensure you have the following on hand as you prepare to mix your magical drinks:

→ **Cocktail shaker:** A stainless steel or glass container for mixing ingredients. Ice is added to the smaller half of the cocktail shaker before shaking. (Look for a shaker with a built-in strainer.)

→ **Jigger:** A double-ended tool used for measuring a "pony" jigger, or 1 ounce (at the small end), and a standard jigger, or 1½ ounces (at the large end) of liquid. Be aware that jiggers come in a variety of sizes and measurements, but in these recipes, we will use a standard jigger measurement of 1½ ounces.

- **Peeler:** Primarily used for creating garnishes.

- **Small cocktail knife:** Used for flaming peels, a knife is crucial as it allows for access to the white pith of the fruit, producing more essential oils to create a little flame.

- **Muddler:** A stick made of wood or plastic that is perfect for breaking down herbs and fresh ingredients in a drink, allowing their oils and juices to release into the alcohol. (The back of a spoon can also be used as a muddler.)

- **Bar spoon:** A long spoon used to stir and layer drinks. Its long neck allows for easy, quick maneuvering.

- **Mixing glass:** A glass used to stir drinks with ice instead of shaking them, so that the resulting cocktail is still cold, but not as aerated or frothy as a shaken drink.

Once you have all your tools, it may be useful to enchant them, if desired, to add an extra layer of magic to them. For a simple, quick enchantment, light cinnamon incense and pass your tools back and forth through the smoke. Envision the enhancing energy of cinnamon enchanting your tools with extra potency. You can do this beforehand each time you create a cocktail.

THE DRINKWARE

After collecting your potion-making tools, the next step will be the glassware. There are a lot of vessels on the market for your enchanted creations, but if you are just beginning your journey into magical cocktail making, it is best to focus on the most common glasses. These are the glasses you will use in the recipes in Part 2:

- **Old-Fashioned (also "Rocks" or "Bucket") glass:** Holds 6–8 ounces; designed for "building" drinks (adding each ingredient and stirring the contents in the glass).

- **Cocktail (or "Martini") glass:** Holds 3–5 ounces; designed for drinks mixed in a shaker and strained into a glass without ice.

- **Highball (or "Collins") glass:** Holds 8–16 ounces; designed for tall drinks that contain a large proportion of nonalcoholic mixers poured over ice.

- **Margarita glass:** Holds 10–16 ounces; designed for margarita cocktails or other fruity drinks.

- **Hurricane glass:** Holds 15–20 ounces; designed for tropical drinks such as a Piña Colada.

- **Irish coffee glass (or "Irish coffee mug"):** Holds 6–12 ounces; designed for hot beverages.

- **Champagne flute:** Holds 6 ounces; designed for carbonated beverages.

- **Coupe glass:** Holds 4–6 ounces, designed for aesthetic cocktails.

- **Red wine glass:** Holds 8–12 ounces; designed with a balloon-shaped bowl to release the aromas of the wine.

- **White wine glass:** Holds 8–12 ounces; designed with a slim bowl to preserve the temperature of chilled white wine.

- **Pint glass:** Holds 16 ounces; designed for beer.

When your crafting station is fully stocked with the essential tools and glassware, you are almost ready to mix drinks like a professional. However, before taking on the title of magical mixologist, there are a few key terms you will want to review.

BARTENDING TERMS AND TECHNIQUES

When it comes to mixing drinks, there are certain techniques that go a long way toward making your magical cocktails pop. The following are the popular terms and tricks you will encounter when creating the enchanted libations in Part 2:

- **Double straining:** Using both a hawthorn strainer and a mesh strainer. The hawthorn strainer catches the bigger bits of ice and fruit/herb particles while the mesh strainer catches the finer particles. This technique allows for a smoother, cleaner beverage for sipping. Hold the hawthorn strainer against the shaker or mixing glass with one hand and the mesh strainer just above your selected drinking glass with the other hand. Now pour the drink into the glass.

- **Expressing a peel:** Using a knife or peeler to cut the peel of a citrus fruit, holding the peel above the cocktail (the rind facing the drink), and squeezing either side of the peel so that the oils from the rind shoot out onto the drink. As a bonus, rub the expressed peel against the rim of the glass so that any remaining oils lend extra aroma as you sip. Drop the peel into the cocktail.

- **Flaming or burning a peel:** Expressing the oils of a piece of citrus rind above a lit match, so that the oils briefly catch flame and add a smoky citrus aroma to a beverage. Blow out the flame after lighting the peel. Drop the peel into the drink.

- **Rimming a drink:** Applying salt or sugar to the rim of a drinking glass before pouring the drink. For certain drinks, you can grind up an herb like lavender or rose petals and mix them with the sugar for even more enhanced spellwork. When it comes to salt, you can use a variety of options, such as Himalayan, celery salt, or even black salt for Halloween or for protection. Spicy cocktails usually call for a spiced herb like cayenne pepper mixed in with the salt. To rim a drink, rub a lemon or lime wedge on the outer edge of the cup lip. Spill your selected salt or sugar onto a dish and lightly spin the rim of the glass in the salt/sugar until coated.

- **Rinsing:** Coating the inside of a cocktail glass with a thin layer of alcohol before adding the mixed drink. To do a rinse, simply toss a piece of ice into the glass, then add ¼–½ ounce of your desired alcohol. Swirl the glass with the ice cube and alcohol rinse, allowing it to evenly coat the insides while simultaneously chilling the glass. Then remove the ice cube/alcohol rinse by carefully flicking it out over a sink.

- **Twist:** A twisted strip of citrus peel.

- **Wheel:** A flat, round slice of citrus.

POTION MAKING ON A BUDGET

When it comes to the taste and power of your potions, the quality of the liquors and liqueurs really do make a difference. However, investing in a big bottle of a spirit you've never tried before can lead to wasted money. Consider first purchasing a few small samplers before investing in a full-sized bottle. Additionally, you can create a number of liqueurs and syrups at home for far less using everyday herbs. So allow yourself to get creative while on a budget!

READYING FOR SPELLWORK

With your tools, techniques, and alcohols at the ready, it is time to start mixing magical libations—almost. Before jumping into the enchanted cocktail recipes in this book, it's important to understand the key elements of witchcraft that will enhance (or create) your magic. Devote some time to exploring the herbs, crystals, and other materials you will work with as you mix and enjoy the delicious potions in Part 2. You will also learn how to prepare your workspace and set intentions for effective spells and rituals.

Witchcraft Basics

The craft cocktail world has opened countless opportunities to create magic through the unique energies of different herbs, crystals, seasonal events, and more. While the herbs themselves can be blended right into a potion, other magical elements can be aligned to the beverage to complement or heighten its power.

In this chapter, you will explore all of the magical associations that are key to witchcraft and the cocktails included in Part 2 of this book. From cleansing sage and protective molasses to loving Venus and focusing fluorite, the elements in this chapter will allow you to create your enchanted libations or bring them to the next level. You will also find instructions for preparing your chosen space for witchcraft and setting an intention to ensure your magic is as strong and effective as possible.

MAGICAL ELEMENTS

You have the basics of bartending down, but before you make your drink, it is important to understand the different magical elements you may want to use in or alongside your concoction. In witchcraft, there are various herbs, planetary alignments, crystals, and more that can attune a witch to the energetic web of the universe and enhance the power of their magic. Sometimes this can be as simple as astrological timing—the phase of the moon or the season of the year. Other times, your magic can be enriched through certain items that correspond with your desires. In the following sections, you will explore the special elements that can be used in potion-making magic. While you can certainly dive even deeper into these elements, and read more on other associations not included in these sections, here you will find everything you need to create the cocktails included in Part 2 and elevate their magic even further in the Advanced Magic tips that accompany each recipe.

Astrological Bodies

Witches and nonwitches alike often hear of Mercury in retrograde—a time when communication, travel, and technology all seem doomed. While the appearance of Mercury traveling backward in the sky is just that—an illusion created due to the earth's position in orbit around the sun—this transit, and the positions of the other planets in the solar system, has cosmic influences in our lives. Through attuning a cocktail to a specific planet's energy, you can add potency to your magic or counter the effects of a planetary transit or retrograde. Attuning a cocktail to a planet's energy is as simple as mixing in herbs associated with that planet, enjoying the finished cocktail during the planet's transit through the earth's orbit, or pairing your magic work with a crystal or tarot card connected to that planet. Links to the different planets can also be found and elevated within the astrological signs outlined later in this chapter.

The Sun

The center of the solar system, no one can deny the power of the sun. Responsible for all light and life on earth (alongside water), the Sun represents self-expression, identity, ego, and consciousness. Ruler of the astrological sign Leo, attuning magic to the Sun can be extra potent in magical efforts for success, triumph, charisma, stage presence/attention, and creativity. While the time of day (dawn, noon, and dusk) is due to the earth's rotation as it orbits the sun, these times of day can also add potency to any magical workings.

The Moon

Perhaps the second most influential astro-logical body in the sky, the moon and its beauty has featured prominently in human poetry and mythology throughout history. Ruler of the astrological sign Cancer, the Moon manages emotions and intuition. It pokes and prods the inner psyche and guides our emotional natures. The first phase of the moon, the new moon, is believed by some to be a good time for rest and relaxation. Others believe it is a good time to do manifestation work. Following the new moon, the waxing moon symbolizes growth and is perfect for efforts of manifestation. The full moon is sometimes utilized for the raw magical emo-tion and power it can induce. Other times, it can be utilized for self-care and cleansing. The waning moon is used in workings that involve decrease.

Mercury

Infamous in modern culture due to the phe-nomenon of Mercury Retrograde, the planet Mercury rules communication, travel, and technology. The ruling planet of Gemini and Virgo, Mercury relates to how one thinks, organizes, and communicates ideas. Connec-ting to the energies of Mercury can help you in magical efforts involving these areas.

Venus

Venus is the planet of pleasure. It inspires love, creativity, art, beauty, and balance. Ruling the signs of Libra and Taurus, Venus loves creature comforts and things that are aesthetically pleasing. This planet deals with how people relate to one another, and also material abundance and prosperity. It can be used in magic involving love, finance, aesthe-tics, and glamor.

Mars

Associated with war and agriculture, Mars is the ruler of physicality and temperament. As its rulership of Aries may indicate, all matters pertaining to aggression and physically energy relate to this astrological body. Mars is about physical competition and sexuality—how one's vitality and life force is physically expressed and exerted. Attune your cocktail to Mars for energy, passion, fire, and matters involving competition and vitality.

Jupiter

Jupiter is the planet that opens doors and grants luck and new opportunities. Reflecting its rulership of the sign Sagittarius, Jupiter symbolizes philosophy and humor. Its generosity and optimism can be harnessed in spells to turn luck and fortune, and also in opportunities of higher education. Jupiter also brings about justice and a sense of morality.

Saturn

Ruler of karma and time, the planet Saturn rules the energy around government and restriction. Saturn is a planet of order and law enforcement. Sometimes harsh, it can be ruthless in unveiling unpleasant realities, but all with the purpose of growth. Saturn reminds you of where your restrictions are. Saturn rules Capricorn and can be a particularly useful association in workings involving time and structure/order.

Uranus

With a sudden bolt of surprise, the ruler of Aquarius can shake and stir things up. Represented as revolutionary and seemingly erratic at times, Uranus brings about necessary changes through the breaking of rules and regulations. This "suddenness" also relates to random sparks of genius and intuition. The occult and future technology are this planet's domain. Use the energy of Uranus to empower workings involving sparking genius and breaking free from a confining situation.

Neptune

Ruler of the sign Pisces, Neptune represents the element of mystery and the unknown. Neptune brings hazy dreams and inspiration but can also reach far into ungrounded areas and cause illusion and a lack of connection with reality. Neptune is the realm of the mystic; it inspires spirituality and enchantment. Use Neptune as companion to magical cocktails invoking imagination, fluidity, and psychic dreaming.

Pluto

With its intense transformative energy, Pluto is no doubt the ruler of Scorpio. Ushering in extreme metamorphosis, and ruler of death and rebirth, Pluto brings about endings but also new beginnings. These themes of life and death, power and change, make Pluto related to shamanic endeavors. Attune to Pluto's energy during magical workings that involve death and extreme transformation.

Astrological Signs

Throughout the calendar year, the sun traverses a number of major constellations. The position of the sun at the time of a person's birth determines their sun sign. These astrological sign seasons provide a specific energy, and the meaning behind the signs can be utilized within your magical cocktails for powerful spellwork. To include an astrological sign in a chosen cocktail, you may either select herbs associated with that sign to mix into the drink itself, enjoy it during that sign's astrological season, or pair it with a crystal or tarot card that elevates the sign's energy. Magical connections to the signs can also be found and enhanced through the planets outlined previously in this chapter.

Aries: March 21–April 19

The first sign of the astrological year, ambitious Aries gets things moving—and moving quickly. Ruled by the planet Mars, this pioneering fire sign pushes ahead through uncharted territory. Aries is a prime initiating force, opening up new opportunities, forward movements, job promotions, prosperity, and health.

Taurus: April 20–May 20

Coinciding with the holiday of Beltane or May Day, it makes sense that Venus-ruled, earth-based Taurus invites energy for growth, beauty, and abundance. Grounded in the physical plane, Taurus is a sign of practicality but also of physical comforts. It is a time of craving and nurturing the basics of survival, and the drive to ensure you have all you need for physical life and the enjoyment of that life.

Gemini: May 21–June 20

Mercury-ruled Gemini finishes off spring and ushers in summer with an emphasis on communication. An air sign, Gemini is quick-thinking and full of information. This is a key time to socialize and share ideas but also to have fun while doing so. Gemini energy appreciates excitement and can get bored very easily.

Cancer: June 21–July 22

Ruled by the Moon and the water element, Cancer provides a key opportunity for self-care and healing in the midst of a lot of outward-focused energy. Nurturing Cancer reminds you to take care of yourself in order to be successful and happy in the future.

Leo: July 23–August 22

Following the nurturing, emotional energy of Cancer comes creative and strength-oriented Leo. Ruled by the Sun and the fire element, Leo is all about making one's mark on the world. This is a time for self-expression and success, and for empowerment and confidence workings. Be honest about yourself, and don't be afraid to shine.

Virgo: August 23—September 22

Mercury-ruled Virgo is associated with straightening things up. What kind of information do you need? How do you need to prepare and get organized to truly achieve your dreams and aspirations? Earthy Virgo focuses on the details, being more efficient, and planning ahead.

Libra: September 23–October 22

Ruled by Venus, loving Libra balances the scales. After the season of critical, organized Virgo, this air sign comes at the first touch of fall, bringing release, calm, and love. Libra is a time to invite balance into your own life and embrace love and beauty.

Scorpio: October 23–November 21

Scorpio season moves away from the loving, social energy of Libra into the intense, transformative death-and-rebirth energy of watery Scorpio. This is the time when you face unpleasant truths, inner darkness, and deep wounds in order to undergo metamorphosis. Ruled by Pluto, Scorpio is an extreme sign.

Sagittarius: November 22–December 21

In the season of Sagittarius, you move away from Scorpio's intense pursuit of inner, dark truths into new ideologies and enthusiasm. Jupiter-ruled Sagittarius transforms the lessons of Scorpio into fresh ideas and experiences. Creative, adventurous, and inquisitive, fiery Sagittarius asks the big questions in life regarding meaning and purpose.

Capricorn: December 22–January 19

After the philosophical, adventurous Sagittarius season, Capricorn invites stability, ambition, and practicality. It's no surprise then that this rational earth sign is ruled by Saturn, a planet focused on discipline and efficiency. This is a wonderful time to take the ideas and purpose-oriented energy of

Sagittarius and put together a business plan for life. How can you take those big ideas and create grounded, practical change? Capricorn's earthy ambition and materialism can help propel you into a successful future.

Aquarius: January 20–February 18

Following grounded, practical Capricorn season comes the innovative, expansive energy of Aquarius. An air sign ruled by insightful Uranus, Aquarius stimulates ideas, playfulness, and freedom from bonds, and can reveal ways in which people limit and constrain themselves. What belief patterns and ideas about life are actually preventing manifestation? How can you expand your worldview to open to more possibilities? Aquarius invites innovation and creative approaches to problems and desires.

Pisces: February 19–March 20

Ruled by Neptune and the element of water, Pisces invites alignment with spirituality. Attuned to the collective consciousness, Pisces also welcomes contemplation and meditation. This is a time to dream and aspire. Boundaries can be difficult with Pisces energy, but this confusion allows for inspiration that will greet the beginning of spring.

Wheel of the Year

In many modern witchcraft practices, the Wiccan Wheel of the Year is utilized as a way to celebrate the changing of the seasons and their metaphorical and symbolic influences in a witch's life. In the following sections, you will discover each important event in the Wheel of the Year. To use these events to complement or heighten the magic of your enchanted cocktails, you may mix and enjoy the cocktail during a certain day/night of the year or select herbs for your drink that are associated with that event.

Ostara/Spring Equinox

Ostara brings the rekindling of life and fertile energies into your spiritual life. Coinciding with the spring equinox, Ostara is a fertility festival. Similar to Mabon, this day is one of equal daylight and darkness. Henceforth, the days will be longer than the nights.

Beltane/May Day

May 1 welcomes another famous pagan holiday, called Beltane. Also known as May Day and featuring traditional elements like the maypole, this is a day of fertility. On this day, sensuality and creativity are celebrated. Many marriages occur around this time in addition to healing, purification, and youth rites.

Litha/Summer Solstice

Greeting the entrance to summer is the celebration of Litha. A solar festival, it is the longest day of the year. From this day, the days will begin to wane in their length, signaling an eventual turn of the seasons. Agricultural themes take center stage on this day, as well as those of power and purpose.

Lammas/Lughnasadh

The last holiday of the summer months is known as Lammas, and it is also one of the first harvests of the year. Also known as loaf mass, this day signals a key change in the season and preludes the coming fall and season of death. It is a time of blessing and payments of debts, for each grain harvested is a seed of promise for the spring.

Mabon/Autumn Equinox

The greeter of fall, Mabon celebrates the autumn equinox. One of two days of the year where there is an equal amount of daylight and darkness, Mabon represents balance. It is also the celebration of the second of the three harvests occurring between the end of summer and the middle of fall. Mabon is a time to balance and ground, and give thanks and offerings for abundance.

Samhain/Halloween

No witch's holiday is more famous than Samhain. A celebration of death, ancestry, and the final harvest of the harvest season, Samhain is a time of transformation. Heightened by occurring in the midst of intense Scorpio season, Samhain is both a time of darkness and a time to seek wisdom. Around this date, many cultures worship the dead, and it is believed this time is when the veil between the living and the dead is the thinnest.

Yule/Winter Solstice

In the midst of the cold, dark months comes the longest night of the year: the winter solstice. Yule is a celebration of the rebirth of the sun and the promise of days to grow longer and more fruitful. Projects and ideas begin to advance, and the rest of astrological winter can be spent on gathering information and developing skills to promote their growth and success in spring.

Imbolc

The last holiday of winter, Imbolc is a fire festival that celebrates the returning of the light and invites in spring. At Imbolc, halfway between winter solstice and the spring equinox, days are becoming noticeably longer and there is the promise of renewal, abundance, and growth in the air. It is a time for purification and clearing.

Moon Phases

There are few depictions of witches as familiar and ancient as the dance under the full moon. To this day, witches gather with friends under the light of the moon or charge their crystals and water in its energy. The new moon's magical energy is strongly tied to the astrological sign and season during which it occurs. As you become more familiar with witchcraft cocktails, you can create your own libations based around the energy of a certain moon.

Chakras

Chakras are concentrated areas of energy within the body. In modern western spiritualism, there are seven main chakras, each correlating to different aspects of your life. The flow (or lack of flow) in a chakra center affects how well those elements of your life are currently flourishing. Because different magical elements are aligned with certain chakras, you can use these elements to make cocktails that can boost a blocked chakra, or use the open energy of a chakra to heighten a spell or ritual relating to its themes. Crystals, for example, are often linked to specific chakras. Look for these chakras in the other magical elements of this chapter, and the recipes in Part 2.

Root Chakra

The root chakra is located at the base of the spine and is generally represented as a red wheel or rotating ball of light. Being the closest to the earth, this chakra is all about grounding. It deals with issues involving security, safety, and survival, and thus can tie into wealth, income, and heritage.

Sacral Chakra

The sacral chakra is located right below the naval and is depicted as a ball or wheel of orange light. Given its proximity to reproductive organs, this chakra correlates to themes of gender, creativity, vitality, and sexuality.

Solar Plexus Chakra

Along the spine, right beneath the breastbone, is the solar plexus chakra. It is represented by a yellow wheel of light. This chakra typically deals with connection to oneself—to confidence, willpower, and overall understanding of who you are. Themes revolving around happiness and self-esteem also arise within this chakra.

Heart Chakra

The heart chakra is found along the spine, right by the heart. This chakra is represented by a green wheel of light. The heart chakra is about compassion, connecting to others, and happiness, and it can indicate how open you are to giving and receiving energy.

Throat Chakra

The throat chakra is represented by a blue wheel of light, and is located at the base of the throat. This energy center deals with communication and self-expression.

Third Eye Chakra

In the center of the forehead is the third eye chakra, depicted by a purple wheel of light. This chakra deals with intuition and perception as well as harmonious thinking.

Crown Chakra

The crown chakra is located on the top of the head, and it is represented by a white wheel of light. It is all about wisdom and connection to the divine.

Crystals

Imparting strong vibrations, crystals are a wonderful enhancement to any magical cocktail. Each crystal has unique powers and associations. You can use them by holding them while drinking your concoction, by pointing them down at your cocktail while envisioning the result, or by infusing alcohols or syrups with them. In the following sections, you will discover details about each powerful crystal used to elevate the magic of the recipes in Part 2.

Amethyst

Associated with the crown and third eye chakras, amethyst connects you to the divine and to spiritual wisdom. It is perfect for developing intuitive abilities while also providing auric protection. A wonderful stone for stress relief, amethyst helps break addictive patterns and also invites peaceful rest.

Ametrine

Ametrine combines the metaphysical energies of citrine and amethyst, allowing for calm insight and positive energy. It also invokes balance due to this duality.

Black Jasper

Black jasper (linked to the root and solar plexus chakras), also known as basanite, promotes stability. It can be particularly useful for those experiencing spaciness, and may also help connect you to higher vibrations in the earth for potent manifestation work.

Blue Apatite

Blue apatite is linked to the third eye and throat chakras, and aids psychic abilities and accessing knowledge. It is a great stone for dreamwork and astral projection, and its connection with vision makes it a powerful ally for past life work and accessing karmic issues.

Blue Calcite

Blue calcite is associated with the throat and third eye chakras, hinting at its psychic and communication-enhancing energies. However, blue calcite is also a wonderfully soothing stone, helping the mind to calm, release stress, and embrace more positive thinking. In this function, it can be useful for inviting clear intuition and problem solving.

Blue Kyanite

Blue kyanite enhances psychic abilities such as dreamwork and astral projection. It stimulates the transfer of energy, helping to open all the chakras and promote energy flow. It is also believed to help link the physical, astral, and causal bodies to promote full consciousness in the day-to-day.

Blue Lace Agate

Blue lace agate is a powerful communication stone. Tuning you into your higher self, this stone will help invite calm and relaxation, but also assist with mental clarity.

Blue Sapphire

Activating the third eye and throat chakras, blue sapphire is a stone of awareness and discipline. It helps quiet the mind to uncover hidden truths, inner wisdom, and visions of what the soul really wants. Its connection with the throat chakra promotes speaking this truth into reality. Blue sapphire's association with the planet Saturn also makes it a great ally for magic work around organizing ideas and turning them into a reality.

Carnelian

In ancient times, carnelian was believed to invoke courage and boldness. In addition to aiding with these leadership qualities, it promotes physical vitality and energy, and it is helpful in taking that first step or having the energy to pursue your dreams.

Chiastolite

Chiastolite (linked to the sacral and root chakras) is an eye-catching stone that features a distinct black cross pattern. Often called a cross stone or fairy cross stone, chiastolite is connected to the four cardinal points (north, south, east, and west). This correlation promotes the flow of chi (energy), manifesting balance, health, and harmony. This stimulation of flowing energy also makes chiastolite useful for removing old thought patterns and sparking new ideas and creativity. Chiastolite is a protective stone that's particularly helpful in warding off negative energies and perceived curses.

Chrysocolla

Chrysocolla is a heart and throat chakra stone, making it wonderful for communicating with compassion and expressing suppressed emotions and/or thoughts. It has a gentle, loving energy that is also associated with femininity. It helps to stabilize and release fear.

Citrine

Citrine transmutes negative energy into positive energy. This stone will help connect you to inspiration and creativity, as well as invite joy and happiness.

Fluorite

Fluorite is known as a focusing stone, helping to clear the mind of debris. In this way, fluorite helps soothe anxiety and worry. It is a wonderful stone for students, and for focusing intention and productivity.

Garnet

Garnet connects you to the energies of survival and draws repressed emotions to the surface, allowing you to recognize them and heal. In attuning you to your instincts, garnet reminds you of what motivates you. It will help feed the fire you need to pursue your aspirations.

Grape Agate

A type of purple chalcedony that forms in round groupings, grape agate is named for its spherical, purple clusters reminiscent of grapes. It is associated with psychic enhancement, especially lucid and prophetic dreaming. Its ties to the crown chakra also inspire stability and calm, while its appearance signifies royalty, wealth, and luxury.

Green Kyanite

Green kyanite has especially strong ties with the heart chakra and nature. It helps you tune in to your intuition in order to discover your inner truth. Green kyanite also helps you connect to the flow of chi (energy) in the universe, making it a great stone for magic centered around balancing and equalizing.

Hematite

A root chakra stone, hematite is a powerful grounder and protector. Its heavy weight connects you to the earth's energy, and its gentle vibration balances and soothes. Hematite absorbs negative energy, protecting you against the emotional highs and lows of others.

Honey Calcite

A sacral and solar plexus chakra stone, honey calcite is a powerful crystal ally for connecting to your personal power. This makes honey calcite great for magic work surrounding confidence, persistence, creativity, and sensuality. Once in an empowered, centered state, you can explore the depths of your being to promote joy and success.

Jet

Associated with the root chakra, jet is a calming and grounding stone. Jet acts like an energetic filter, clearing out negative emotions and energy, making it great for empaths. Formed from compacted, fossilized wood (with similarities to coal), jet provides insight and wisdom in any magic work.

Lapis Lazuli

Lapis lazuli is a marvelous ally for psychic development and clear communication. This stone will help you access other realms and communicate with your guides. Lapis is ideal for psychic journeys for this reason, and it can also be used to journey within oneself to uncover and heal karmic cycles.

Lodestone

Lodestone, also known as magnetite, is typically used in witchcraft for its natural magnetism that makes it great for attracting something to you. Its connection to the polarity of the earth also makes lodestone wonderful for grounding and aligning the chakras.

Mahogany Obsidian

Mahogany obsidian can assist in clearing ancestral patterns and other limitations. It is a wonderful stone to work with for moving away from a mindset of scarcity into one of abundance.

Malachite

Associated with the solar plexus and heart chakras, malachite consciously connects you with your inner power and shows you how to express that power in constructive and creative ways. It helps ground your ideas and open your mind to discern what steps are necessary to turn your dreams into a reality. Malachite also helps you recognize what boundaries are necessary for ourselves and others.

Moonstone

Moonstone (linked to the third eye and crown chakras) helps you connect to your higher self and intuition, inviting calm understanding. A powerful stone commonly used for aligning to Goddess energy, moonstone invokes creativity and inner power. Magic workers also use moonstone to promote safe travel and help balance emotions.

Morganite

A sparkling peach-pink crystal, morganite opens up the heart chakra to both universal love and wisdom from the divine. Whether doing love divination or inducing romance, morganite can help manifest love in your life. It is also useful in spells surrounding the psyche.

Nephrite Jade

A powerful healer, nephrite jade is often used to increase the speed of the healing process. Associated with the heart chakra, it helps to open you to life's abundance and transmute any blockages in the path to prosperity. Wear it for good luck, to balance your energies, or to aid in any healing.

Peridot

Peridot is a powerful personal growth stone. It connects the wearer to universal love, helping to heal and remove blockages within the ego, thereby opening you up to joy, prosperity, and the ability to share. Peridot is a powerful ally for abundance and heart healing.

Petrified Wood

Technically a fossilized piece of tree or other vegetation, petrified wood is a grounding root and sacral chakra "stone" that can help connect you to the wisdom and strength of the past. For this reason, petrified wood is particularly useful for magic work involving communication with ancestors, as well as karmic and past life regression work.

Pink Calcite

Associated with the heart chakra, pink calcite connects you to divine love and helps clear obstacles in your emotional expression. Pink calcite inspires wholeness and empathy, and helps provide emotional support as it clears away negative energies and feelings.

Pink Opal

Pink opal (linked to the heart chakra) aids in self-acceptance and love. It is particularly powerful in breaking negative energy patterns to allow more joy into your life.

Quartz

Quartz is a perfect stone for programming, and will amplify any intention you set with it. Use quartz for clarity and to enhance memory.

Red Jasper

Its ability to strengthen chi makes red jasper a wonderful healing and stabilization stone. It promotes soft, slow changes to build the foundation for more permanent and enduring change.

Rose Quartz

Rose quartz connects you with universal love. This beautiful pink stone is about loving oneself and recognizing the beauty within and all around. Rose quartz invites peace, comfort, and gratefulness.

Rutilated Quartz

Featuring golden lines of rutile captured in clear quartz, rutilated quartz is a powerful amplifier that works with all chakras and is thus ideal for manifestation. Infusing the wearer with light energy, it can be used for connecting to the divine, channeling creativity, or for psychic communication. Its illuminating energy can also be cleansing and balancing to all chakras.

Sea Jasper

Linked to the solar plexus, heart, and throat chakras, sea jasper is a stone of joy and high spirits. It is a particularly powerful stone for working with cellular memory, where energy patterns are often stored, allowing you to access and change these patterns. In this way, sea jasper helps you make positive changes in your life and to see things from a more positive perspective.

Selenite

Selenite is a crown chakra stone, wonderful for connecting to the higher vibrational, angelic realms and to your own higher self. Known for its cleansing and protective properties, selenite will also keep any space, person, or item energetically clean.

Shungite

Connected to all seven chakras, shungite is a powerful stone for protection from electromagnetic frequencies (EMF) and for clearing auras, as well as one's emotional body, of any negative energy. It also helps integrate and activate the light body to balance and align.

Smoky Quartz

Associated with the root chakra, smoky quartz is a grounding stone that helps anchor energy, making it a wonderful choice for integrating higher energies into your physical body, or inviting healing frequencies after energy magic. Smoky quartz is also a great choice for protection or when dealing with pain, since it absorbs negative, lower vibrations.

Tigereye

Tigereye assists with willpower. It helps you to build confidence in yourself and to see through deception. Connected to both the sun and earth, tigereye invites balance and power.

Turquoise

This throat chakra stone is associated with honest, clear communication and spirituality. Turquoise helps you bring together all the elements of your "self," embrace your past through a new point of view, and imagine the infinite possibilities of the future.

Tarot

Tarot is a form of divination that uses a deck of cards depicting archetypal themes of life. The Major Arcana in tarot contains twenty-two trump cards, each representing a unique character. The Minor Arcana in tarot contains fifty-six cards, divided into four suits—each with a corresponding natural element and themes: Wands (fire; action, passion, and creativity), Pentacles (earth; career, money, and family), Cups (water; love, spirit, and emotion), and Swords (air; communication, ideas, and success). The magical associations of different tarot cards can be used to bring the power of your enchanted cocktails to the next level. You can reflect on the themes and imagery of a card as you mix or sip your beverage or place the card under the mixing glass itself as you add ingredients. The tarot cards outlined in this section and used to enhance the recipes in Part 2 are from a standard Rider-Waite deck. Not all of the cards in tarot are included in this section; instead, you will find descriptions only for those cards mentioned in Part 2. Feel free to explore the other tarot cards and work their themes into your own cocktails.

The High Priestess

The High Priestess is represented by a woman robed in a long blue cloth with a crescent moon at her feet and pomegranates behind her. She rests between two columns—one black and one white—and is holding a scroll of wisdom in her hands. The High Priestess represents the balance of dark and light and the idea of feminine wisdom and intuition. She symbolizes reorganizing priorities and personal power.

The Empress

The Empress represents nurturing and abundance. Depicted as a pregnant female with a fertile garden around her, she symbolizes creativity and the time to give birth to something new. The energy of the universe is promising for new endeavors and dreams. This card also points to a close connection to nature.

The Lovers

A man and woman stand at either side of The Lovers card, a red-winged angel hovering above them. The tree of Eden, laden with apples and a coiled serpent, graces the background. The Lovers card is about alignment and dual forces coming together. This can symbolize two people with deep physical attraction or love, or alignment with one's own destiny.

Strength

The Strength card represents triumph and success. Featuring a woman holding open a lion's mouth with her hands, it symbolizes victory over difficult tasks, or that a gentle energy can mend a challenging situation. It can also represent physical health and vitality.

The Hermit

The Hermit depicts a cloaked man heading down a path with a guiding lantern in his hand. This can symbolize a need to retreat, but it is also about spiritual wisdom and getting in touch with your inner light and purpose.

Wheel of Fortune

The Wheel of Fortune card shows a wheel with various symbols hovering in the sky. A sphinx holding a sword sits on top of the wheel. The Wheel of Fortune reflects the element of change. It is about life's ups and downs. It can also mean energy is still forming about a situation, and magic may be useful to intervene. The Wheel of Fortune card embodies luck, good fortune, and chance happenings.

Death

An armored skeleton sits atop a white horse on the Death card. The skeleton carries a flag in one hand as the horse tramples people below. The Death card is about the ending of a cycle or relationship, bringing about transformation and the beginning of something new and different.

Temperance

Depicting a winged figure pouring water from one cup to another, the Temperance card is about patience, balance, and divine timing. It can symbolize present harmony or waiting for a situation to pass.

The Tower

The Tower card shows a lightning bolt hitting the top of a tall tower on a cliffside. The tower is catching fire, and its occupants are thrust from the building as it burns. The Tower represents destruction. It can symbolize an argument or drama, but also that something in your life is unstable and may not be built to last. There is a sense of loss and confusion within this card, but it also offers an opportunity to rebuild and restart with something better.

The Star

The Star shows a woman kneeling with one foot on land and one foot in water. She pours water into the pool and onto the earth as she kneels. A large star shines in the background. The Star card follows The Tower card and symbolizes a deep healing and connection to your spiritual self. It is about being vulnerable—alignment to your destiny occurring as a result.

The Moon

Depicting two wolves howling up at a moon, The Moon card can mean a sense of confusion and mood swings. It depicts a desire or need for clarity, but it also symbolizes a deeper need to connect to your soul for guidance.

The Sun

On The Sun card, a child crowned in flowers sits atop a white horse and waves a long flag. The Sun brings blessing and effective communication. Things are looking up, and success can be had. It also reflects a sense of happiness and contentment.

The World

The World card depicts a woman floating in the sky, holding batons or wands in either hand. Surrounding her in a perfect circle is an evergreen wreath, and four different archetypes/spirits in each corner: a person, a bird, a bull, and a lion. It represents limitless possibilities; one cycle may be coming to an end while another is beginning.

Ace of Wands

On the Ace of Wands, a cosmic hand offers a firm and stable wand above a plentiful land. This card is about new creativity, new passion, and offers. It represents success and a new physical relationship.

Two of Wands

The Two of Wands shows a man atop a tower, holding a globe in one hand and a wand in the other. This card represents planning ahead from a stable vantage point—a place where foresight is possible.

Nine of Wands

Nine of Wands depicts a person holding on to a wand in front of a wall of other wands. This card symbolizes preparing for battle, rest and retreat before a final battle, and eventual victory.

Page of Wands

A man gazes at a wand on the Page of Wands card. This card is about plentiful creative ideas and planning.

Knight of Wands

The Knight of Wands shows an armored knight sitting atop a sprinting horse, holding a wand in his hand. This tarot card symbolizes fast movement as well as passionate thrill and excitement.

Ace of Pentacles

As the first card of the pentacle suit, the Ace of Pentacles represents new beginnings and blessings in the areas of money, kinship, and career. It depicts an outstretched hand offering a large pentacle coin above a rose-covered arch.

Two of Pentacles

The Two of Pentacles shows a man wearing a large hat, balancing two pentacles in an infinity symbol. This card is about balance and juggling things so as not to be overwhelmed.

Four of Pentacles

The Four of Pentacles features a man with a crown who clasps a coin pentacle in one hand, with another pentacle atop his head and two below his feet. This tarot card represents financial security and a wealth of opportunities that lie ahead.

Nine of Pentacles

The Nine of Pentacles depicts a man adorned in a luxurious robe, with a bird perched on his outstretched hand. This card represents financial independence and plentiful wealth stemming from hard work.

Ten of Pentacles

The Ten of Pentacles shows an inner and outer view of a small kingdom. An elderly man surrounded by pentacles pets two dogs. This card is about family, and a kingdom with money and blessings that manifests from a financial or career pursuit.

Knight of Pentacles

The Knight of Pentacles shows a knight holding a coin astride an unmoving horse, a full landscape unfolding in front of him. This card is about long-term financial gain and investments, as well as stability, hard work, and determination.

Ace of Cups

The Ace of Cups depicts an outstretched hand offering a cup overflowing with water and a blessed dove, above a body of water that contains lilies. This card symbolizes new beginnings, either in your emotional life or aligned with a particular soul path. It can mean a new relationship or the opening of yourself to the possibility of a new relationship, as well as new opportunities and new beginnings in love and life.

Two of Cups

The Two of Cups depicts two people sharing and trading cups. It represents equal balance and sharing in a relationship, as well as mutual love and attraction, or alignment within a job or life path that has a perfect balance of spiritual and physical energies.

Three of Cups

The Three of Cups shows three women dancing atop a bountiful earth, with glasses raised. This card symbolizes celebration, good news and good luck, and the abundance that comes from harmony, working together, and relationships.

Six of Cups

The Six of Cups depicts an adolescent passing a plant-filled cup to a child. This card emits energies of nostalgia, childhood, and more importantly, the blessings and healing that come from childhood.

Ten of Cups

Two children and two adults rejoice beneath a rainbow of cups in the sky on the Ten of Cups card. This card is about happiness, marriage, and celebration among a group of people. It reflects happiness and blessings to come.

Queen of Cups

The Queen of Cups card shows a woman sitting on a throne holding out a cup in offering. This card symbolizes intuition, connection to one's emotion, and heart healing.

Ace of Swords

The Ace of Swords depicts a hand holding a blade adorned with a crown. This card is about swift action, clarity, cutting through the fog of confusion, and accomplishment, along with the determination to overcome obstacles.

Edible Elements

When it comes to witchcraft cocktails, the magical associations of herbs, fruits, and other edible elements take center stage in creating a dynamic and powerful beverage. In this section, you'll discover the common herbs and their magical, planetary, and elemental associations. Many of these edible elements can be included in your enchanted cocktail recipes through the use of bitters, shrubs, and syrups, as you will discover in Chapter 4. Others may be added to cocktails in their raw form. When choosing your own edible elements for a cocktail, trust your intuition, using this section as a guide for your instincts.

Agave

Also known as maguey, agave is a relative of the asparagus plant. It blooms once every ten to twenty-five years, after which it quickly dies and must be harvested fast for its sap to make tequila and mezcals. Since agave has such an interesting life cycle, it can be a great plant to use in magical workings or cocktails related to honoring the dead or transformation. Magically, it is associated with the planet Mars and the element of fire, and these connections make it wonderful for love, sex, and lust workings. Since it is produced from a late-blooming flower, agave is also perfect for magical workings involving beauty and youth, as well as for coming into your power.

Almond

Almond is associated with money and prosperity, as it is a more expensive element. Tied to the element of air and the planet Mercury, almond is also used in success, wisdom, and healing magic.

Anise

With its strong smell, anise is excellent for protection, youth, and purification. However, it can also be used to connect to spiritual energy and power in divinatory work and to manifest lucid dreaming and dream recollection. It is linked to the planet Jupiter and the magical element of air.

Apple

Attuned to the planetary energy of Venus and the magical element of water, apple has long been used for healing, fertility, and longevity. When horizontally cut, the apple displays the customary pentagram of magic: five points that represent the four elements plus spirit. Apple also has long-standing magical associations with divination practices and wisdom.

Apricot

Associated with Venus and water, it is no surprise that apricot is strongly linked to love, and it is often used as an offering to the goddess Aphrodite. Apricot is also used in magic to "sweeten" people up, or win them over.

Basil

Basil is a wonderful heart-opening herb that blooms midsummer into autumn. It has a strong association with love and was once used as a token of affection. Its strong aroma associates it with protection as it cleanses the air and invokes clarity and wisdom in decision making. Basil calms the nerves and helps bring in harmony and prosperity. It is associated with the actionable planet Mars and the passionate element of fire.

Bay Leaf

Connected to the radiant energy of the sun and the element of fire, bay leaf is a multidimensional herb, strengthening your psychic powers and prophetic dreams while offering protection from negativity. It is also used for wisdom, wishing, success, purification, strength, and healing. Bay laurel leaves are particularly popular around Yule/winter, although as a dried herb, they are available year-round in grocery stores.

Bergamot

Bergamot is a type of orange that is commonly used in Earl Grey tea. It is associated with the planet Mercury and the element of air, and it is particularly useful in workings involving money and clarity.

Blackberry

Blackberry is a multipurpose plant due to its thorny vines, abundant leaves, and juicy, dark berries. The fruit at the end of a protective plant, it shows the beauty of what can be accomplished with some protection. It is a popular late summer/harvest fruit for Lammas/Lughnasadh celebrations, and its preservation through wines and jams has been also used at Imbolc and considered sacred to the goddess Brigid. When used for Brigid, blackberry becomes transformative and healing. Blackberry is tied to the loving energy of Venus and the psychically attuned element of water. It is also useful in magic work surrounding money.

Blueberry

Blueberry is associated with the energies of protection—specifically psychic protection, due to its connection to the moon and the magical element of water. Additionally, it can be utilized to represent prosperity and abundance.

Cardamom

Associated with the planet Venus and the element of water, cardamom is a popular lust-inducing herb. It promotes love and sex, and is easily added to coffee or tea and baked into pies.

Chamomile

Chamomile is well known as a sleep-inducing and relaxation herb (chamomile tea, anyone?). A summer and fall herb linked to the sun, Mercury, and the element of water, it is very grounding and allows for healing, enhancing dreamwork and aiding in divination. It is also used in money workings, and for clarity, communication, and luck.

Cherry

Magically attuned to the planet Venus and the element of water, cherry has strong associations with love. It can be used to stimulate love and happy unions, and to increase fertility. Cherry is also a symbol of abundance and can be used for attracting good luck. The pits are used in divination rituals.

Chili Pepper

Chili pepper is known for its hot flavor. Associated with the planet Mars and the element of fire, it can be used to reignite the heat in a relationship. It is also useful for breaking spells and ushering away negative energy.

Chrysanthemum

Though delicate in flavor, chrysanthemum is not an herb to underestimate. Associated with the sun and the element of fire, this flower is a powerful agent of strength and protection from negative energies. It is also used for ancestor worship during Samhain.

Cinnamon

Cinnamon is a powerful spice. Connected to the vibrant energy of the sun and the bold element of fire, cinnamon easily raises the magical vibration of all things, making it perfect for spirituality and situations in which someone needs fast luck. It is used for enhancing personal power and also adding a bit of zest to love and sex magic. Cinnamon sticks are often included in abundance rituals, and ground cinnamon is sprinkled for protection in the home. Cinnamon is a go-to spice for almost anything, including creativity, divination, and healing!

Clove

Clove is a wonderful wintertime spice beloved for its enlivening, comforting flavor. Associated with the planet Jupiter and the element of fire, clove is used for abundance, raising spiritual vibrations, attracting a love interest, and driving away unwanted energy.

Cocoa

Cocoa, or chocolate, helps induce a sense of emotional well-being and happiness. It also opens you up to love and can be utilized for increasing prosperity. It is associated with the planet Mars and the element of fire.

Coffee

Many people, including witches, begin their day with a fresh cup of coffee to revitalize their energy and mental alertness. Coffee grounds and beans have been used for divination as well. Coffee is associated with physical energy as well as the mind, divination, and uncrossing workings. It is connected to the planet Mercury and the element of fire.

Cranberry

Cranberry is largely associated with protection and is often eaten for such. However, due to its red color, it is also used in spells for love and abundance. Associated with action-oriented Mars and the passionate element of fire, cranberry can also be useful for magical workings involving setting and following through with goals.

Cucumber

Magically connected to the moon and water element, cucumber is great to work with for beauty and youth magic, as reflected in its popularity in modern beauty rituals. It has strong associations with feminine energy and is used for healing and mending the body.

Elder

The elder plant in general is associated with the planet Venus and the element of water. It is used to connect to fairies and nature spirits, and to elevate the power of spells and healing. Elder is also associated with protection and warding off evil energies and negativity. It produces both berries and flowers that are utilized in teas and other items.

Eucalyptus

A favorite in aromatherapy, eucalyptus enchants the air with its soothing scent. This wonderful herb is associated with the moon and the elements of water, and is great for magic work that involves healing and protection.

Ginger

With such a strong flavor, it is not surprising that ginger is associated with the bold planet Mars and the passionate element of fire. It is used in a variety of spells, including those for love, success, power, and healing.

Grapefruit

Grapefruit is a strong purification fruit associated with the sun and the element of water. It is a terrific fruit for lifting up one's mood and warding off depression and negativity.

Hazelnut

Hazelnut is associated with wisdom, divination, and protection. It is used to aid in various magics, and its connection to the sun, Mercury, and the element of air make it perfect for promoting creative ideas. It is also a wonderful choice for protection magic.

Hibiscus

Associated with Venus and the element of water, hibiscus is a potent herb in magic work surrounding lust, love, and divination. A stunning blossom, hibiscus lends a floral note and sensual red-pink hue to your cocktails.

Jasmine

Jasmine is associated with love, money, and prophetic dreams and powers. It is a popular herb for love and self-care—in particular for love of a spiritual natural. Jasmine's connections with Mercury, the moon, and the element of water also enhance its communication and divinatory abilities, such as channeling, astral travel, or dreamwork. It is also associated with abundance and money.

Juniper

Juniper is the potent herb that makes a gin, a gin. It is added either before or after the distilling process, or sometimes both, to infuse the mixture. An herb of the sun and associated with the magical element of fire, juniper is a powerfully protective herb used to guard against evil and negativity. It purifies a space and also helps enhance divination, dreamwork, and psychic ability. Juniper is also useful in immortality and longevity magic.

Lavender

Lavender is one of the most popular herbs for witches—and everyone else too! Associated with the planet Mercury and the element of air, lavender's scent induces relaxation, which paves the way for calm, clear thinking. For this reason, lavender is used for peaceful sleep and is also found in a variety of healing rituals and beauty items. Its ability to reduce mind chatter also makes lavender perfect for all forms of psychic work. In addition, it is a wonderful aid in love and protection magic.

Lemon

Lemon is an accessible, cleansing go-to for witches. Associated with the moon and the element of water, it works as a wonderful energy cleanser for places and items, and also to promote social energies and positivity within friendships. Lemon's vibrant flavor and energy also bring good luck.

Lime

Lime is a potent fruit for protection; associated with the sun and the magical element of fire, its bold flavor and energy can be used to repel ill wills and hexes, and protect against the evil eye. Alternatively, it can also be used for healing and love.

Maple

Maple is associated with the planet Jupiter and the element of air, and it is often used to induce a long life, love, and money. Its heavy, hearty flavor make maple great for grounding, while its sweetness as a syrup can be useful for abundance and "sweetening people up" so as to win their favor and/or affection.

Milk

While not an herb, milk can be a strong addition to your magical endeavors in cocktail mixing. Associated with the moon and the element of water, milk is wonderful for connecting to goddess energies and for manifesting fertility and beauty. Its nourishing energy makes it great for love workings as well, and its divine nature (and the fact that it was once given as an offering to the gods) makes milk strongly associated with spirituality.

Nettle

Associated with Mars and the element of fire, nettle can be used to promote lust and also protection or reversal (moving negative energy back to its sender). It was once sprinkled around the home to repel evil. Nettle is also great for healing and is known as an adaptogen that will correct a variety of nutritional imbalances.

Nutmeg

Nutmeg is associated with Jupiter and the element of fire. A popular wintertime herb, it is warm and comforting, and primarily used for good luck, health, and money.

Onion

Associated with Mars and the element of fire, onion has long been used for protection, exorcism, and healing. Well known in pop culture for being a repellent of vampires, onion can be used to protect a person from negative energy. It is also used to this day to help assist healing when sliced into quarters and placed around the home.

Orange

Orange is associated with the sun and the element of fire. As reflected by the morning ritual of drinking orange juice, it is tied to happiness and energy—an energy that induces internal purification. This energy is very spiritual, connecting orange to spiritual love and making it a wonderful fruit to use with friends and family as a mood enhancer. Orange also has magical associations with luck and money as a symbol of abundance.

Papaya

Native to Central America, papaya has been used for a vast number of wellness remedies. It has potent enzymes for regulating digestion, is believed to enhance beauty, and also has a magical association with love. In some cultures, papaya was even utilized as an aphrodisiac, making its association with the moon and the magical element of water no surprise.

Parsley

Parsley is another traditional garden herb that offers a multitude of magical uses. Associated with Mercury and the element of air, parsley can enhance the energies of fertility and lust, protection and purification, and can also help stop misfortune.

Peach

Sweet peach isn't just a great addition to cobbler. This Venus-associated fruit has long been used for love, happiness, health, and wisdom. In particular, peach has been used for longevity in Chinese lore. Peach can be used to help expand your ability to give and receive love and even to win over someone's heart. Peach is also associated with fertility in Japan, and it is believed to have been used for divination and purification as well.

Peppermint

Peppermint is a type of mint that offers similar but distinct magical and taste offerings to its relative spearmint. It is related to Mercury and the element of fire, making it wonderful for communication, psychic development, and purification. It is also perfect for remedying stomach and throat maladies as a tea, and so it has associations with healing. Peppermint can also be used for money, travel, and sleep.

Pineapple

A popular tiki drink ingredient, pineapple is associated with the sun, Mercury, and the element of fire, and is known to inspire happiness. Also a popular decor element, pineapple symbolizes hospitality and kindness. It is used for healing and to bring in money, protection, and love. Its solar association makes it a wonderful addition in spellwork focused on happiness, creativity, or success.

Pomegranate

Famous for its plentiful seeds and blood red juice, pomegranate offers energies of divination, wealth, and fertility. It is also often used in spells as a replacement for blood. Vital, nourishing pomegranate is associated with Mercury and the element of fire.

Pumpkin

A fall favorite, pumpkin is associated with the moon and the element of earth. Abundant and plentiful with the cooler harvest season, pumpkin invites the energies of healing, money, and abundance into magic work.

Raspberry

Associated with passionate Venus and the emotional element of water, it's no wonder raspberry so easily invokes happiness and love when used in spells. It is a deliciously romantic addition to magic.

Rose

The rose has long been a symbol of femininity and beauty in Western traditions. However, its association with Venus and the element of water carry it far beyond the physical realm. Rose can be used to assist magic work involving psychic ability, healing, luck, and even protection.

Rosemary

Rosemary is associated with the sun and the element of fire. An herb of many talents, it is first and foremost a powerful cleanser of energies. It can drive away negative energy so that you can enjoy peaceful sleep, but it is also great for knowledge, psychic ability, and memory.

Saffron

A more expensive spice that packs a strong punch in small amounts, saffron is magically associated with the sun and the element of fire. As such, it is a wonderful herb for lifting someone's mood and inviting happiness. Saffron's solar association makes it ideal for work involving strength and healing, and it can also be used for lust, love, and psychic powers.

Sage

Sage is one of the first herbs many modern witches are introduced to for cleansing. In the kitchen, however, we use culinary sage. This herb, associated with Jupiter and the element of air, is used for wisdom and protection magic. Drinking sage tea is said to promote longevity and wisdom that opens you up to the power of the divine and to psychic channels.

Spearmint

Like all mint, spearmint can be used to help sharpen the mind and is also helpful in protection spells. It is associated with Venus and the element of water, making it great for healing and love magic as well.

Strawberry

A summertime favorite, strawberry celebrates the change of seasons and can invoke happiness, love, and harmony. It is often used for stimulating love interest, but its sweetness invites harmony into any relationship. Strawberry is also wonderful for good luck and is associated with the element of water and the planet Venus.

Sugarcane

Sugarcane is associated with the planet Venus and the element of water, hinting at its strong abilities in magical workings of love and lust. Its sweetening energy also helps to displace negative energies and can aid in purification and protection work.

Thyme

Thyme is a garden witch's must-have herb, with numerous talents and magical associations. Connected to the planet Venus and the element of water, thyme is particularly useful for sleep, healing, inducing love, and enhancing psychic powers. It is also used to invite vitality and courage, and when burned can help clear a space for healing work.

Vanilla

A more expensive spice, vanilla is associated with money and abundance. Connected to the planet Venus and the element of water, vanilla is used for love, peace, and seduction. It is also believed to provide energy and assist the mind by encouraging clear and precise thinking.

Violet

A beautiful indigo blossom with an enchanting scent, violet isn't just a part of Valentine's Day rhymes. Associated with the planet Venus and the elements of both air and water, it is great for magical workings involving love and healing. It can also be used to enhance sleep and psychic work. Often blooming at the end of winter to greet the spring, violet invokes a sense of hope, and as such can be used to change luck and remind you of the coming season of the fae folk.

Walnut

Associated with the sun and the element of fire, walnut offers far more than a protein-filled snack. In witchcraft practices, walnut can be used to invoke wisdom, mental clarity, and healing.

YOUR OWN UNIQUE TWIST

Part of what draws many people to witchcraft is its versatility. We all have our own flavor preferences (sweet or acidic, ice or no ice, more alcohol or less alcohol) and approaches to how we practice magic. After you get a handle on mixing drinks, feel free to experiment and add your own unique twist to the cocktail recipes in Part 2. Just be sure to consult the proper use of each herb before adding. In the back of the book, you'll find an appendix with different magical intentions and the ingredients associated with each. Use this to help you combine ingredients and flavors. There are also recipes for classic cocktails in the appendix that you can use as a base to make your own special witchcraft cocktails.

SETTING INTENTION AND PREPARING YOUR SPACE

Once you've explored the magical elements of witchcraft, the first step to creating your own magical potion—whether a cocktail or simply a tincture—is to become clear on your intention. What is the purpose of this magical elixir? Is it to win someone over within your job? To manifest new friendships? To induce a night of passion? Or

inspire success and courage in your pursuits? Select key words surrounding this theme (and perhaps create a physical list of them to keep track), then create a positive statement about your goal(s). Magic follows the path of least resistance, so the phrase for successful magic should not be spoken from a place of lack or fear, but rather as if it is already true and happening right now. For example, instead of, "I want more money," you can say, "Money flows easily and freely to me" or "Money rains on me and comes from all directions and unexpected places."

Once you have your affirmation or positive statement in mind, the next question to ask is whether the beverage itself is a single magical effect or part of a greater spell or cumulative magical effect. A cocktail that is a magical effect in itself, for example, will induce a specific outcome. It may be a love potion or money-making spell. Cocktails that are part of a greater magic would be used either before or in unison with a spell or ritual to increase the power of that magic, or enjoyed afterward to reaffirm the enchantment. They may also be used to ground you or cleanse your energy after magic work. The answer to this question will determine any other materials you may need and how the magic will be executed.

Aligning Ingredients

Now that the purpose of the cocktail is settled and key words established, it is time to choose ingredients that align with your selected spell or ritual. All of the ingredients (as well as bartending items and magical elements) you will need for the recipes in Part 2 are listed accordingly. However, if you wish to create your own magical potion using magical elements not found in this chapter, books like *Llewellyn's Complete Book of Correspondences* (by Sandra Kynes) and *Cunningham's Encyclopedia of Magical Herbs* (by Scott Cunningham) are invaluable resources. You can also use the appendix at the end of this book to assist you in your selections.

When first working with witchcraft and magical cocktails, it is best to begin with the ingredients and energies illustrated within the recipes in Part 2. Following a bit of practice, you can experiment with your own ingredients and energy focuses if desired.

Attuning Ingredients

Part of your magic work with cocktails will include attuning the ingredients to the intention you set before beginning a chosen spell or ritual. The recipes in Part 2 provide specific instructions for attuning the ingredients used. However, if you are creating your own magical cocktail recipe, here is a simple guide for attuning any ingredient:

1. Place the ingredient in your hands, put your hands on either side of a container holding the ingredient, or hold your hands above the ingredient.

2. Close your eyes and take a few deep breaths in through your nose and out through your mouth. Draw your attention to the expansion of your belly as you breathe.

3. Once you feel focused, move your attention to your hands, and see if you can sense an "energetic tingling" coming from the ingredient. Or, simply imagine a light glowing and tingling within the magical element. Reflect on any specific visuals, ideas, or feelings within the ingredient.

4. Now, visualize your desired outcome. Imagine yourself glowing as a result of this visualization, and that glow seeping into the ingredient itself until it too grows brighter with the energy of your intention.

Preparing Your Space

When your intention is set and ingredients and energies identified, prepare a space for your witchcraft. (This will happen before you gather the ingredients and witchcraft and bartending tools needed for the spell.) You will first cleanse the area, so that any unwanted or lingering energy from previous use is dispelled. To cleanse the space, add a few drops of sage or lemon essential oil (or spritz the oils out of a lemon peel) to a wet sponge and wipe the surface(s) you will be using when creating your cocktail and completing your spell.

Once the space is cleansed, you will also need to cleanse yourself, to ensure your focus is on the intentions you set and the physical task at hand. To cleanse yourself, slowly run a lemon wedge through the air surrounding your body, then stand over a sink with the wedge in hand. Close your eyes, imagining the lemon holding all your woes and worries, and any negative energy in the room. Now, squeeze the wedge so that its juices fall into the drain, taking the negativity with it. Follow this with washing your hands, perhaps with a little lemon rind oil. Be sure to focus on the sound of the running water, and visualize the faucet purifying any traces of unwanted energy. You can also create a cleansing spray with lemon rinds, rubbing alcohol, and water, and use it to mist the air around your workspace.

Centering and Grounding

Before beginning any magical work, it is important to center and ground yourself. Centering involves bringing your energy and attention back to your physical body, while grounding is about connecting to the earth. To center yourself, take several deep breaths, focusing on your lower belly as you breathe.

Notice how your body feels with each inhale and exhale. To ground yourself, slowly bring your awareness from your lower stomach to the bottoms of your feet. Take a few more deep breaths, noting how it feels to stand and have your feet support your weight and body on this earth.

MAKING YOUR FIRST DRINK

Now that you understand the different alcohols, bartending techniques, and magical elements available to you, and how to prepare both yourself and your space for some potion making, it is almost time to get to work! You may also wish to call upon a helpful spirit or guide by saying something along the lines of "I call upon and humbly ask my spirit guides, allies, and ancestors that nurture my highest good, in perfect love and perfect trust, to come to my assistance in this working. Lend me your powers as I set out to do this work, so that this can be a powerful and potent working for us all." Additionally, you may add the vibrational layers of candles or incense during your spellwork with cocktails.

But before you start gathering your materials and mixing your cocktails, you'll want to explore the following chapter on magical ingredients. These shrubs, bitters, and syrups will add the flavors and enchantments of the herbs illustrated previously in this chapter.

CHAPTER 4

Magical Ingredients

When a witch dresses a candle, packs a mojo bag, or makes a magical mist, they choose corresponding herbs. For harmony, they may select lavender, cornflower, and rose petals. For strength, they may favor bay leaf or saffron. When it comes to bartending, all of those flavors become available in a myriad of delicious ways—not just through liquors and liqueurs, but also in syrups, shrubs, and bitters. You can even choose the type of sugar or vinegar to add for more magical power.

In this chapter, you'll discover more details and simple recipes for bitters, shrubs, and syrups you can use to complement your cocktails and elevate your spellwork. From a Blackberry Shrub to complete a balancing Fiery Mabon Cocktail, to Elderberry Honey Syrup to accent a youthful Playful Fairy, there is a magical ingredient for every occasion.

BITTERS

Long ago, there was no refrigeration. What-ever was not eaten in a short time would simply go to waste, and the different healing herbs and fruits used in witchcraft were only available at certain times of the year and in certain locations, depending on climate. To preserve the essence of these helpful plants, healers made tinctures (condensed essences of herbs preserved in a solvent of alcohol) and shrubs (aged blends of fruit juice, sugar, and spirits). Shrubs, tinctures, and bitters could be kept for months and used in medicines and healing rituals year-round. Even in modern times, bitters have been used in healing. Angostura bitters, for example, were first created by an army surgeon in the early nineteenth century in an effort to quell digestive problems in soldiers.

Bitters have much to offer your magical cocktails. They are so strong that you only need a few drops for each cocktail. While many bitters are available for purchase in stores, you can make your own by steeping selected herbs in a high-proof spirit such as Everclear. Contained in a sealed Mason jar, the herbs and alcohol are shaken every day to keep everything thoroughly mixed. After about one week, taste a drop against the back of your hand to determine the flavor. Some herbs will take longer than one week for the flavor to develop. Once you've determined the flavor is as strong as desired, strain out the solids. Some prefer to discard the solids at this point, while others heat the solids in water, then let them sit for another week before adding the alcohol back in along with sweetener, then straining once more. (The solids would be discarded at this stage.)

SHRUBS

Developed as an alternative to preserving various herbs and fruits, and to quell stomach maladies, shrubs are now a way of adding extra layers of flavor and magic to a cocktail. They are also an easy way to create a quick mocktail. Shrubs typically need to sit from two weeks up to one month before use, to allow for natural bubbles. However, if you don't have time to wait for a shrub recipe to complete, you can add in the bubbles with a little soda water. The following are simple shrub recipes you will use to create a number of the enchanted cocktails in Part 2.

Blackberry Shrub

YIELDS 1 CUP
⅓ cup mashed fresh blackberries
⅓ cup Demerara sugar
5 fresh sage leaves
⅓ cup room-temperature water
⅓ cup apple cider vinegar

Add blackberries, sugar, sage, and water to a small pot. Bring the mixture to a boil over high heat, then pour into a 12-ounce glass Mason jar and add vinegar. Cool for 10 minutes, then cover and store in the refrigerator for 1 week before separating the solids and discarding them. Allow the liquid to sit covered at room temperature or in the refrigerator for another 2 weeks.

Cranberry Shrub

YIELDS 1½ CUPS
1 cup fresh cranberries
4 ounces room-temperature water
½ cup Demerara sugar
1 small fresh sprig rosemary
4 ounces apple cider vinegar

Add cranberries, water, sugar, and rosemary to a small pot. Heat over medium heat for about 5 minutes, allowing the cranberries to pop. Pour the mixture into a 12-ounce glass Mason jar and add vinegar. Cool for 10 minutes, then cover and store in the refrigerator for 1 week before separating and discarding the solids. Allow the liquid to sit covered at room temperature or in the refrigerator for another 2 weeks.

SPELLBINDING SYRUPS

Syrups aren't just for pancakes! In bartending, crafting syrups is a key element of enhancing the flavor of a cocktail. In witchcraft, they lend even more potency to your spellwork. Specifically, sweeteners like syrup have elements of love magic in them, and as alcohol is already an aphrodisiac, a love potion can become that much more powerful when infused with a chosen syrup.

Selecting Your Sweetener

Have difficult in-laws or want to win over your boss at work? In witchcraft, sugar is a notorious way to "sweeten" people up and attract clients and wealth. There are many types of sugars available to elevate your magical cocktails, each lending a unique flavor and energy.

Honey

A natural sweetener, honey is tied to a deep history of goddess worship and spirituality. The result of the hard labor of bees transforming flower nectar into simple sugars, honey can be made from a variety of flowers, all of which result in different colors and flavors. Due to its popularity in homemade beauty products and as a natural antiseptic, honey is magically associated with beauty, healing, youth, and purification. Its long-standing roots in worship make honey a go-to magical sweetener for goddess rituals and workings in love, lust, happiness, and wisdom.

Cane Sugar

The sugarcane plant was grown and harvested for its sweetness as early as 1400 B.C.E. At first, sugarcane was primarily used for natural medicines and preserving food, but with time it was refined to further separate the simple sugars from the plant. Due to its high cost of production, cane sugar was once very expensive and thus associated with wealth, often given as a gift to symbolize love and devotion. Over time, cane sugar has become widely accessible, though it is still used in love and wealth magic. Its sweetening ability also makes it a great option for purification and dispelling negativity, and it can be used as an offering to ethereal spirits and elemental energies.

Agave Syrup/Nectar

Agave syrup is the nectar of the agave plant—the same plant used to create mezcal and (if from the blue agave plant) tequila. Similar to the magical associations of tequila and mezcal, agave syrup is a wonderful boost for love, lust, and youth potions. In craft cocktail bartending, agave syrup is mostly used in tequila drinks, such as a Margarita or paloma, to heighten and complement the agave-based flavors of the alcohol. Given the unique life cycle of the agave plant, agave syrup is perfect for magic involving life/death/rebirth cycles, beauty and youth, love, and coming into one's own power and spirituality (since it is a late bloomer!).

Demerara

A modern favorite among bartenders, Demerara is a light-brown sugar consisting of large granules packed with rich flavor. Demerara sugar naturally holds on to this color due to small amounts of molasses and minimal processing. It is full of deep, grounding flavors, and because of the leftover molasses, it maintains more of the energetic properties of the sugarcane plant, thus making it great for sweetening and protection spells (but also more grounding than ordinary sugar). It is the perfect complement to bourbon- and whiskey-based spirits with limited sugar or citrus in them, such as an Old-Fashioned or Sazerac.

Other Sugars

Every day, new types of sugars are being added to the aisles of your local grocery store. To discover more of the magical properties of a particular sugar such as coconut sugar, for example, check online or refer to a kitchen witchery book for additional guidance.

Crafting Your Syrup

Once you have your sugar selected, it's time to make a magical syrup! In bartending, the typical recipe for syrups is simple: the ratio is always 1:1 of sweetener to hot water (except with agave syrup, which doesn't need to be cut with water). To add some extra magic, you can create a chant while you are readying the syrup or burn a candle for your desired outcome. You can also write your affirmation on a piece of paper or tape and stick it to the outside of the glass before storing in the refrigerator. If you don't have a specific desire, you can simply pray over it to call upon the sweetening power of the sugar. The following are simple steps for a sugar prayer while creating your syrup. You may use this prayer when mixing the syrup recipes noted here:

1. Place the sugar in a bowl, then place your hands over it.

2. Take a deep breath in and then out through your nose and center yourself. Imagine divine white energy flowing from your crown chakra down through your hands and into the sugar.

3. Say: "Sugar so sweet, from something higher. Help sweeten the world to my desires." As you speak, imagine little balls of energy in each grain of sugar growing brighter and brighter with the infusion of your words. You can add herbs as well at this time.

Lavender-Chamomile Syrup

Hazelnut-Chamomile Bourbon

Elderberry Honey Syrup

Hibiscus-Rose Honey Syrup

Simple Syrup

Simple Syrup is an easy, go-to recipe used as a sweetening agent in a variety of cocktails, from Whiskey Sours to Old-Fashioneds.

YIELDS ¾ CUP
½ cup granulated sugar
4 ounces boiling water

Place sugar in a 12-ounce glass Mason jar or small bowl. Pour in water, and stir until the sugar is dissolved. Let it cool for about 5 minutes. Place syrup covered in the refrigerator until ready to use, up to 2 weeks.

Grenadine

Grenadine is a popular bar syrup used in cocktails such as the Tequila Sunrise and mocktails like the Shirley Temple. It has a deep red color and a flavor that is both tart and sweet, which makes it a favorite. Traditionally, Grenadine is made from pomegranate juice. Pomegranate is used for its magical properties in creativity, money, death, fertility, luck, and wishes.

YIELDS 1½ CUPS
1 cup pomegranate juice
½ cup granulated sugar
4 strings saffron, crumbled
1 teaspoon orange blossom water

Heat a medium pot over medium heat for 30 seconds. Add pomegranate juice and sugar. Stir continuously until sugar is dissolved, about 5 minutes. Add saffron and let the mixture reach a slight boil, then remove from stove and let cool for 15 minutes. Add orange blossom water, then transfer to a sealable container and store refrigerated for up to 2 weeks.

Honey Syrup

Honey Syrup is a great way to introduce the sweetness of flower nectar into your cocktails. It is used in classic cocktails like the Bee's Knees and the Hot Toddy.

———— ◆ ————

YIELDS ⅞ CUP
½ cup pure honey
4 ounces boiling water

Place honey in a 12-ounce glass Mason jar or small bowl. Pour in water. Stir until the honey dissolves, and then cover and place in the refrigerator until ready to use, up to 2 weeks.

Elderberry Honey Syrup

With the sweet, fruity combination of elderberry, elderflowers, apple, and honey, this syrup is great in love workings and for communication with the spiritual world. Apples and the elder plant are both domains of the love goddess Aphrodite. Apple is often used in purification and fertility rights as well. Steeped in smooth, sweet honey, this syrup whispers of attraction and abundance.

———— ◆ ————

YIELDS ⅞ CUP
1 tablespoon dried elderberries
1 tablespoon dried elderflowers
1½ tablespoons peeled and cubed red apple
⅓ cup hot water
⅔ cup pure honey

Place elderberries, elderflowers, and apple in a 12-ounce glass Mason jar. Place your hands around the jar, imagining the hum of bees awakening the herbs to the energies of love, excitement, and the attraction of the natural world. Pour hot water over the herbs, and let steep for 5 minutes. Add honey. Refrigerate covered for at least 24 hours, strain, then store for up to 2 weeks in the refrigerator.

Bergamot-Ginger Syrup

Bergamot, a citrus tied to money and clarity, is one of the prominent flavorings in Earl Grey tea, making it a very accessible blend for herbal syrup. Ginger is an herb of many talents, offering love, money, success, and power. It heats up love and is associated with curing various illnesses. It also adds a lovely, complementing spice to the bergamot of the Earl Grey tea.

YIELDS ¾ CUP
1 Earl Grey tea bag
1 tablespoon chopped fresh ginger
4 ounces hot water
½ cup granulated sugar

Put tea bag and ginger in a 12-ounce glass Mason jar. Place your hands over the jar and concentrate on the powers of the herbs—on the clarity and money-providing energy of bergamot and the awakening, invigorating energy of ginger. Pour hot water over tea bag and ginger, and let steep for 5 minutes. Pour in sugar and mix until all the sugar has dissolved. Refrigerate covered for at least 24 hours, strain, then store for up to 2 weeks in the refrigerator.

Vanilla Syrup

Vanilla's potent flavor soothes the mind and inspires love, balance, and wealth. This easy, beautifully smooth Vanilla Syrup is a great way to call on the magical uses of vanilla in love and peace magic, as well as for money workings.

YIELDS ¾ CUP
4 ounces room-temperature water
½ cup granulated sugar
1 (1"-long) vanilla bean

In a small pot over high heat, boil water. Pour sugar into a small bowl. Hold vanilla bean between your hands and tune in to its energy. Smell it and visualize your energies mixing with the herb's. Now imagine your desired outcome, and a little light waking the vanilla bean up with abundance and peace. Use the bean to draw a heart in the sugar. Add the hot water and bean and stir until sugar is dissolved. Pour the mixture into a 12-ounce glass Mason jar and cover. Label the syrup "love and peace." Refrigerate for up to 24 hours, then remove and discard vanilla bean. Store covered syrup in the refrigerator for up to 2 weeks.

Lavender-Chamomile Syrup

This sweet herbal syrup comes packed with nuanced flavors of two of the most popular herbs in the kitchen witch world. Together, lavender and chamomile inspire cleansing and relaxation. A mercurial herb, lavender also purifies and protects, while chamomile is commonly used to soothe stomach problems and remove negative energy.

YIELDS ⅔ CUP
1 tablespoon dried lavender flowers
1 tablespoon dried chamomile flowers
4 ounces hot water
½ cup granulated sugar

Place lavender and chamomile in a 12-ounce glass Mason jar. Place your hands over the jar, closing your eyes as you imagine the grounding, relaxing essence of the herbs. Envision a small light within the herbs opening them up and growing bright with your intention. Once the herbs feel energetically juiced, pour hot water over them and steep for 5 minutes. Add sugar and mix until sugar is dissolved. Let cool for 10 minutes. Place covered in the refrigerator for at least 12 hours, up to 2 weeks. Strain when ready to use.

Jasmine-Cinnamon Honey Syrup

With just a dash of energizing cinnamon, this soothing jasmine syrup will inspire creativity and abundance. Associated with the moon, jasmine is known for bringing spiritual awareness that induces prophetic dreams and sleep. Cinnamon raises the spiritual vibrations of this syrup and is also commonly used for fast luck and success.

YIELDS ½ CUP
2 cinnamon sticks
1 tablespoon dried jasmine flowers
⅓ cup hot water
⅓ cup pure honey

Place the cinnamon sticks and jasmine in an 8-ounce glass Mason jar. Cupping the jar, close your eyes and bring your awareness to the herbs. As you notice their subtle energies, think of your intention and imagine small seeds of light appearing within the herbs, growing brighter and brighter. Once you feel the herbs charged with energy, pour hot water over them. Allow the herbs to steep for 5 minutes before mixing in the honey. Cover and place in the refrigerator for 24 hours, then strain and store for up to 2 weeks in the refrigerator.

Nettle-Hyssop Syrup

Nettle is a powerful herb for cleansing, hex removal, and protection. An adaptogen, it also provides a variety of nutrients to the body. This is a great syrup to use in physical healing concoctions or for energy, protection, or changing your luck. It can be enhanced by the addition of lemon, saffron, or peppermint, and has a refreshing, minty flavor.

YIELDS ¾ CUP
4 ounces room-temperature water
1 tablespoon dried nettle leaves
1 tablespoon dried hyssop
½ cup granulated sugar

Boil water in a small pot over high heat. While waiting for the water to boil, gather nettle and hyssop in a small bowl. Place your hands above the bowl, and close your eyes while taking a few deep, centering breaths. Tune out the world around you, and bring your awareness to the palms of your hands and the herbs in the bowl. Then, decide on an intention. Say a chant or affirmation if desired. Pour the hot water over the herbs and steep for 5 minutes. Add sugar and stir until the sugar is dissolved. Allow to cool for 10 minutes, then strain and refrigerate covered for up to 2 weeks.

Bay Leaf—Orange Syrup

Bay leaf is a great cleansing, healing, and success-oriented herb. It is also popular for wishing spells and is burned for wisdom and psychic ability. This is a wonderful syrup for cleansing work, strength, success, and wishes.

YIELDS ⅞ CUP

4 ounces room-temperature water

2 dried bay leaves

1 large orange peel

½ cup granulated sugar

In a small pot over high heat, boil water. While waiting for water to boil, hold bay leaves and orange peel between your hands in the prayer position. Think about the intention for the syrup, say a few words or chant if desired, and imagine a light growing within the bay leaves in your hands. Rub your hands together slightly, then put leaves and peel in a 12-ounce glass Mason jar and pour in the hot water. Allow to steep for 5 minutes, then add sugar and stir until dissolved. Let jar sit covered in the refrigerator for 24 hours. In the morning, as the sun rises, remove the bay leaves and orange peel. Use as desired.

Hibiscus-Rose Honey Syrup

This delicious syrup is sure to sweeten anyone to your favor. With hibiscus and rose steeped in honey, it is a potent addition to love, spirituality, and self-care potions.
It also adds a light-pink color to your cocktails.

***

YIELDS ¾ CUP
4 ounces room-temperature water
½ tablespoon dried hibiscus flowers
½ tablespoon rose petals
½ tablespoon rose hips
½ cup pure honey

In a small pot over high heat, boil water. While you wait for water to boil, place hibiscus, rose petals, and rose hips in a small bowl. Place your hands over the top of the bowl, and take a moment to connect to the dormant energies of sweet hibiscus and rose. Visualize your intention, and push the feeling into the herbs. Once you feel a resonating, energetic buzz, withdraw your hands and draw a heart with your finger in the air above the herbs, or into the herbs with a spoon. Add the hot water, thinking of the magical energies of the herbs spreading out into the water. In a 12-ounce glass Mason jar, add honey. Allow to steep for 5 minutes, then pour the rose mixture into the jar and stir. Let cool for 10 minutes, then cover and refrigerate for at least 4 hours, up to 12 hours. Strain the herbs and store for up to 2 weeks in the refrigerator.

Rosemary-Saffron Syrup

What is a witch's garden without rosemary? Utilizing the myriad energetic benefits of the herb paired with radiant saffron, this syrup is wonderful in a number of magical cocktails for strength, wisdom, power, and healing.

YIELDS ¾ CUP
4 ounces room-temperature water
½ cup granulated sugar
2 strings saffron
1 small fresh sprig rosemary

In a small pot over high heat, boil water. While bringing water to a boil, place sugar in a 12-ounce glass Mason jar and tune in to its sweetness and capacity to win over any energy. Set aside. Add the hot water to a separate bowl. Sprinkle saffron into the hot water while visualizing drops of the sun's rays, then pour the water into the jar. Now hold rosemary between your hands and pray. With intention, use rosemary to mix the syrup. Slowly, visualizing its energy mixing, drop the sprig into the jar and pray. Store covered in the refrigerator for 24 hours, then remove the rosemary and saffron from the mixture, and keep refrigerated for up to 2 weeks.

INFUSIONS

Alcohol preserves the vibration and essence of any ingredient, including those that are magically charged. Along with shrubs, bitters, and syrups, alcohol infusions are one of the simplest ways to incorporate the energy of enchanted herbs into your cocktails. And they are even easier to prepare than shrubs or bitters!

How to Infuse

To create your own infusions, simply choose an herb or peel (fresh or dried) and let it sit in the alcohol. Taste the infusion every few hours until it reaches the desired flavor intensity. Different herbs take unique amounts of time to infuse, and some will be stronger than others regardless of the length of time they are infused. Vodka is the most popular alcohol for infusing, due to its neutral flavor, but you can infuse other types of alcohols too. Chamomile gin, clove brandy—the possibilities are endless. The following are simple recipes for magical infusions you will use for different cocktails in Part 2.

Hazelnut-Chamomile Bourbon

Inspired by summer harvests, this Hazelnut-Chamomile Bourbon combines light, floral chamomile with nutty hazelnut in a relaxing, grounding bourbon base. It's a perfect infusion for communication, divinatory potions, and celebrations of summer.

—◆—

YIELDS 2 CUPS
½ cup whole hazelnuts
1 tablespoon dried chamomile flowers
2 cups bourbon

Mix hazelnuts and chamomile flowers together in a small bowl and place your hands over the bowl. Visualize little lights brightening inside of the hazelnuts and flowers. Carefully make a knocking motion with one hand above the herbs, as though waking them up from their slumber. Pour the mixture into a quart-sized glass Mason jar, and add bourbon. Cover and store in a cool, dark place for about 6–10 hours depending on flavor preference. Remove the hazelnuts and flowers. Store for up to 3 months.

Jasmine Gin

With the combined cleansing aspects of juniper and jasmine, this infusion is wonderful in cocktails involving love, cleansing, and spirituality magic work. Gin itself is a go-to alcohol in exorcism/banishment efforts, as well as for cleansing and psychic development.

YIELDS 1 CUP
1 tablespoon dried jasmine flowers
8 ounces gin

Place your hands over the flowers, either between your palms or in a clean bowl. Close your eyes and take a deep breath to center yourself. Imagine white light pouring through you from your crown chakra at the top of your head all the way down to your hands. Envision the essence of the flowers bathing in this light and opening up. When you feel an energetic response from the flowers, place them into a 12-ounce glass Mason jar, and with a quiet mind, pour gin over them. Cover and store in a cool, dark place. After 1 hour, strain out the jasmine and save for a later date. Store for up to 3 months.

PART 2
Magical Cocktails

CHAPTER 5

Fall Cocktails

As the heat of summer wanes and the grain harvests begin, the earth slowly retracts her energy within her core. The last maturing herbs and fruits are plucked from the fields, and all life begins to slow down. Fall is a time of culmination, a period when the witch focuses on reaping the last of their manifestation efforts and begins to turn inward. It is a season of celebration and hard work—of death and transformation—and a time to recognize lineages and those who walked the earth before you.

The recipes in this chapter harness the reflective, celebratory energies of fall to create complete spells, or enhancing aids in any magic work you practice. And while they are associated with the fall season, their power can be carried over into witchcraft any time of the year. From a sparkling Charmed Leaf for protection, to an herbal Black Cat for luck, there is an enchanted libation for any occasion.

Persephone's Descent

With the turning of the season to fall, the Greek goddess Persephone begins her descent into the Underworld to reign as queen for the next six months. As she shrouds herself in the shadows of Hade's dark realm, witches explore and embrace their own shadow side during this season. This is a time to shed old skins and turn inward to discover your own truth. Utilizing Persephone's signature fruit, the pomegranate, this cocktail can invoke the insight and enchantment of the shadows. Replace tequila with mezcal for a smokier version of this drink.

Energies: *Divination, Fertility, Beauty, Strength*

SERVES 1

Black salt, to rim glass
2 tablespoons (1 ounce) silver tequila
1 tablespoon pomegranate liqueur
1 tablespoon pomegranate juice
1½ tablespoons lime juice
1 tablespoon agave syrup

Rim a margarita glass with black salt. In a cocktail shaker, add tequila, pomegranate liqueur, pomegranate juice, lime juice, and agave syrup. Add ice and shake. Strain into prepared margarita glass.

ADVANCED MAGIC

The High Priestess

The High Priestess is a tarot card of introspection, and can represent the wisdom that can be found in embracing and acknowledging the darkness within. Like Persephone, The High Priestess balances the dark and the light. As you sip this concoction, contemplate both Persephone and The High Priestess tarot card. What might these archetypal figures have in store for you during fall?

The Black Cat

While some superstitions may insist that black cats are bad luck, witches and hoodoo practitioners believe otherwise. Associated with a positive change in luck, black cat oil (no cats are harmed in the processing of this oil!) is used to invoke favorable chance outcomes.

A modified Toronto cocktail, this concoction is sure to turn fortune in your favor! For a sweeter version, increase the syrup amount by ½ tablespoon. Garnish with fresh sage.

Energies: *Reversal, Luck, Wishes, Spirituality*

SERVES 1

½ tablespoon anise liqueur

1 large fresh sage leaf

2 dashes Angostura bitters

½ tablespoon Nettle-Hyssop Syrup (see recipe in Chapter 4)

⅛ teaspoon activated charcoal

1 jigger (1½ ounces) rye whiskey

1½ tablespoons Fernet-Branca

In a coupe glass, add 1 ice cube and anise. Rinse the glass with anise liqueur and set aside. Tear sage leaf into a mixing glass, imagining that you are ripping any negative luck or hexes away. Add bitters, syrup, and activated charcoal to mixing glass. Muddle sage leaves, again visualizing any negative energy in your life being torn apart. Add rye and Fernet-Branca, then ice to fill ¾ of mixing glass. Stir the cocktail counterclockwise, saying, "Black cat, black cat, come my way. Invoke a change of luck today." Now stir clockwise, closing your eyes and repeating the words. Stir until the drink is chilled, visualizing good luck entering your life. Empty anise rinse from the coupe glass and strain your potion into the glass, imagining plentiful blessings coming your way as you pour.

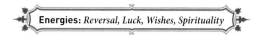

ADVANCED MAGIC

Wheel of Fortune

The Wheel of Fortune card often symbolizes good fortune and chance happenings. Utilize the energies of the Wheel of Fortune to inspire positive change and luck. As you stir this cocktail, keep the card nearby to help visualize your stirring as the wheel of fortune itself, turning ever in your favor.

Fiery Mabon Cocktail

Reflective of grain harvests, the barley malt base of scotch offers a light, smoky flavor reminiscent of summer heat. Featuring the seasonal flavors of blackberry for protection, healing, and abundance, and the wisdom and cleansing of sage, this sacred libation is perfect enjoyed by your Mabon harvest fire or candle while you reflect on your accomplishments thus far, and what you still wish to manifest in the future. And with a little flamed orange peel, you'll reinvigorate what's left of that summer sun into your own personal energy.

Energies: *Wisdom, Healing, Balancing*

SERVES 1

2 ounces scotch

1 tablespoon Blackberry Shrub (see recipe in Chapter 4)

1½ tablespoons Honey Syrup (see recipe in Chapter 4)

2 dashes Angostura bitters

3 fresh sage leaves

1 small flamed orange peel, for garnish

Place scotch, shrub, syrup, bitters, and sage leaves in a cocktail shaker. Holding either side of the shaker, take a moment to think about your intentions for Mabon and the cocktail. Say an affirmation if desired. Add ice, close the shaker tightly, and shake as you reflect on the essence of the harvest contained within. After 5 seconds, strain the cocktail into a highball glass and add a flamed orange peel.

ADVANCED MAGIC

Two of Pentacles

The Two of Pentacles reflects the balance and the changing energy as summer turns into fall. Every cycle will have its end, and now the days are clearly growing shorter, and the autumn breeze is just around the corner. Contemplate the Two of Pentacles as you sip this libation. What needs balancing in your own life?

The Scales

Venus-ruled Libra greets the entrance of fall, inspiring energies of balance, beauty, and artistic inspiration—all autumn associations. With vibrant apple and nurturing Hibiscus-Rose Honey Syrup, this concoction will invite Libra's aesthetic into your life. It's a balanced, fall-inspired cocktail to celebrate the Libra in your own birth chart, wherever it may be! Garnish with an apple slice if desired.

Energies: *Balance, Creativity, Wisdom*

SERVES 1

1 jigger (1½ ounces) hazelnut bourbon

½ tablespoon sour apple pucker

1 tablespoon lemon juice

1 tablespoon Hibiscus-Rose Honey Syrup (see recipe in Chapter 4)

2 dashes Angostura bitters

Place all ingredients in a cocktail shaker. Add ice, shake, and strain into a martini or coupe glass. Place your hands over the concoction, imagining the self-love-inducing and inspiring energies within the cocktail igniting like little fireworks under your palms. For added enhancement, trace the Libra symbol with your fingers above the cocktail.

ADVANCED MAGIC

Pink Opal

To amplify the self-loving energies of Libra, hold a piece of pink opal as you craft and sip this cocktail. This loving stone will heighten Libra's power both within the drink itself and in any surrounding spellwork you may do.

Lunar Libation

Sometimes after a long day, you want a quick way to attune to the energies of the moon before practicing magic. With this simple white wine spritzer, you'll be able to connect with the moon goddess herself (a practice also referred to in witchcraft as "drawing down the moon") and elevate your spellwork. Add lemon bitters for an uplifting note.

Energies: *The Moon, Beauty, Spirituality, Psychic Powers*

SERVES 1

2 thin slices cucumber

10 fresh mint leaves

1 tablespoon Jasmine-Cinnamon Honey Syrup (see recipe in Chapter 4)

3 ounces dry white wine

1 jigger (1½ ounces) soda water

In a mixing glass, muddle cucumber, mint, and syrup. Pour into a stemless wine glass and add wine, ice to fill, and soda water. Stir the cocktail, visualizing the moon's energy being drawn down to you more and more with each rotation.

ADVANCED MAGIC

Moonstone

Moonstone opens the door to the higher self and intuition. A powerful stone for connecting to goddess energy, it invites calm and creativity into your life. It is also a great stone for connecting to the energies of the moon, as its name suggests.
Hold a moonstone while sipping your cocktail, visualizing the moon's light radiating down on you.

Witch's Cosmo

Famous for its pink hue, the Cosmopolitan is an exemplary cocktail of balance. With protective cranberry, cleansing rosemary and lime, and elevating orange, this simply delicious enchantment is all a witch needs to balance out after a long day! Substitute the lime garnish for more rosemary if preferred.

Energies: *Protection, Cleansing, Balance*

SERVES 1

1 jigger (1½ ounces) vodka

1½ tablespoons cranberry juice

1 tablespoon lime juice

½ tablespoon orange liqueur

½ tablespoon Rosemary–Saffron Syrup (see recipe in Chapter 4)

1 small lime peel, for garnish

Place all ingredients except lime peel in a cocktail shaker and add ice. Shake firmly, shaking away the stress of the day and any worries. Once the shaker is chilled, double strain the cocktail into a martini glass. Express lime peel over the top of the cocktail, twist, and drop in.

ADVANCED MAGIC

Ametrine

Ametrine combines the cleansing, positive vibrations of citrine with soothing, mind-clearing amethyst. Hold the crystal above the cocktail with both hands and imagine your intention for cleansing and rebalancing flowing down like light through the crystal and into the cocktail. When you feel an energetic resonance between the cocktail and the stone, sip away.

Blood Moon Margarita

The Blood Moon of October welcomes the time of transformation, and its name perfectly represents what witches and pagans alike honor at this season of the year: the deceased, and the cycle of life and death. Perfect to enjoy around the Blood Moon, this smoky, juicy mezcal Margarita is reminiscent of fall harvests. Its red color connotes its meaning—a period of ancestral connection and the bounty of the earth. Forgo the orange peel garnish if preferred.

Energies: *Transformation, Divination, Death*

SERVES 1
1 jigger (1½ ounces) mezcal
1 tablespoon pomegranate liqueur
1 tablespoon agave nectar
1 ounce lime juice
1 tablespoon blood orange juice
3 pomegranate seeds, for garnish
1 small flamed blood orange peel,
for garnish

Add mezcal, pomegranate liqueur, agave nectar, and lime juice to a martini glass. Add ice to fill, and float blood orange juice on top. Stir briefly. Garnish with pomegranate seeds and flamed orange peel.

ADVANCED MAGIC

Garnet

Garnet is perfect for Samhain and connecting to the deceased. As you reflect on the red color of the drink, gaze upon the similar deep red hues of garnet, held in your other hand. Tune in to its vibration as you sip. Garnet will help strengthen your bonds with the cocktail's energies of grounding, survival, and ancestry.

Clarity Martini

As the name suggests, fall is a time of release. Of course, the mundane acts and dramas of everyday life can make it hard to see clearly and focus your attentions where they are needed. The clarifying energy of vodka, with a little herbal kiss of purifying, mind-enhancing rosemary, can help you shake off the confusion as you move into the transformative cocoon of winter. Enjoy this chilly cocktail as you reorganize your schedule, or to strengthen psychic clarity before or during divination.

Energies: *Clarity, Mental Acuity, Purification*

SERVES 1
½ tablespoon dry vermouth
1 jigger (1½ ounces) vodka
1 small fresh sprig rosemary
1 small lemon peel, for garnish

Place 1 ice cube in a martini glass, pour in vermouth, and set aside. In a cocktail shaker, add vodka, rosemary, and ice, and shake vigorously, imagining any confusion or stress falling away. Once the shaker is cold on the outside, grab your martini glass and give it a swirl to coat the inside with vermouth. Toss out the ice and vermouth. Double strain the vodka into the glass, express lemon peel above the glass, and add peel to the cocktail.

ADVANCED MAGIC

Ace of Swords

Like the Ace of Swords, this cocktail is straightforward and cuts through confusion. Carefully shake your completed potion above the Ace of Swords card, or place the card nearby as you mix. Focus on the sword, envisioning it slicing through chaotic or foggy thoughts.

The Stinging Scorpion

Following balancing Libra comes the Scorpio season of intensity, sex, and transformation—and nothing is sexier and stronger than this twist on the bold Manhattan. The bourbon base contains the essence of the harvest season and its karmic energy, and the vermouth and bitters provide a grounding kick. Delicate chrysanthemum, a Samhain mainstay, ties it all together. Tap in to Scorpio's passionate energy with this tantalizing libation.

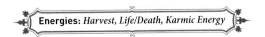

Energies: *Harvest, Life/Death, Karmic Energy*

SERVES 1

1 dried chrysanthemum flower

2 ounces bourbon

1 ounce sweet vermouth

3 dashes Angostura bitters

1 maraschino cherry, for garnish

Fill a martini glass with ice and set aside. Muddle chrysanthemum flower in the bottom of a mixing glass. Pour in bourbon, vermouth, and bitters. Stir the concoction, tuning into the transformative power of three separate ingredients becoming one. Dump out the ice from the martini glass after a quick swirl, and strain the cocktail into the martini glass. Drop the cherry on top to remind yourself that although transformation can be intense, it can also be a good thing.

ADVANCED MAGIC

Mahogany Obsidian

Enhance the powers of intense Scorpio within your cocktail by holding a mahogany obsidian crystal as you sip. Mahogany obsidian can assist in clearing ancestral patterns and other limitations that can arise during this watery scorpion's season. It is also a wonderful healing stone for the root and sacral chakras, helping to open and cleanse them.

The Reaper

Mulled wine is one of the most well-known, long-standing drinks. It dates back to ancient Rome, where wine was cooked and infused with various herbs to help protect against illness and the coming cooler weather. Because of its history, this is a perfect cocktail to make in the fall to accompany a harvest ritual or ancestor worship. Enjoy while sipping by an outdoor fire, or pour some onto the earth as an offering and reflect on all that life has given you. Garnish with a cinnamon stick for added protection.

Energies: *Spirituality, Wisdom, Immortality, Divination*

SERVES 6

1 (750-milliliter) bottle cabernet sauvignon
½ cup pure honey
4 ounces pomegranate juice
3 whole star anise
2 teaspoons ground cinnamon
2 large blood orange peels
4 ounces pomegranate liqueur
1 cup apple juice
1 red apple, sliced crosswise into 6 slices, for garnish

Combine all ingredients except apple slices in a large pot over medium-high heat. Bring to a boil, stirring constantly, then lower the heat to medium and simmer for 10 minutes. Pour into six mugs to share and garnish each with an apple slice.

→ ━━━━━━ **ADVANCED MAGIC** ━━━━━━ ←

Death

The Death card in tarot represents the end of one cycle and the promise of a new one. This card perfectly matches the energy of fall, and also the pomegranate, anise, and apple associations of this cocktail. Reflect on this card as you sip, and think about which cycles may be ending in your life, and which new ones you wish to invoke.

Witch's Cauldron

What's a witch without their mixing cauldron? Based on the infamous Scorpion Bowl, the deep red hue of this fall fruit punch will draw eyes to your magic work. Together, apple, pomegranate, and blood orange offer energies of divination, love, wealth, and fertility. It's a perfect witch's blessing to serve at a party! Garnish with a flamed orange wheel.

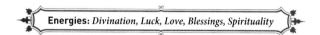

Energies: *Divination, Luck, Love, Blessings, Spirituality*

SERVES 1

1½ tablespoons apple brandy

1½ tablespoons dark rum

1 tablespoon lime juice

1 tablespoon Grenadine (see recipe in Chapter 4)

½ tablespoon pomegranate liqueur

1 jigger (1½ ounces) blood orange juice

1 tablespoon apple juice

Place all ingredients in a cocktail shaker. Add ice and shake until chilled. Close your eyes and breathe deeply as you shake, focusing your intention energy into empowering the ingredients. Strain into a martini glass. Imagine the magical essence of the seasonal pomegranate, blood orange, and apple fusing together as you bless the concoction for all who drink it!

ADVANCED MAGIC

Rutilated Quartz

Rutilated quartz is a crystal of spiritual elevation and manifestation. With golden inclusions of the mineral rutile, this stone brings in elevating energy from the higher self into the material world, invoking positivity, manifestation, and all-around great energy. Use rutilated quartz to imbue your blessing punch with heightened spiritual energy. Gather a few pieces of this crystal and place them with intention around the pitcher or martini glass to allow its vibration to permeate your potion.

The Charmed Leaf

A protective abundance spritzer to celebrate the cold months! Cranberry's red hues are a marker of love, and as a berry, it is also linked to abundance. Cranberries are also traditionally associated with protection. Add grounding maple, and spiritualizing sparkling wine, and you have a sweet potion for grounding and protection magic.

Energies: *Protection, Grounding*

SERVES 1

1 tablespoon Cranberry Shrub (see recipe in Chapter 4)

½ tablespoon pure maple syrup

3 ounces champagne

Pour Cranberry Shrub into a champagne flute. Add in maple syrup, then pour in champagne. As the champagne bubbles up and fills the glass, imagine a bubble of spiritual protection surrounding you.

ADVANCED MAGIC

Black Jasper

Also known as basanite, black jasper is a lower-chakras (root, sacral, and solar plexus) stone that promotes stability. This stone is a wonderful energetic companion for The Charmed Leaf cocktail, to be used before or after engaging in spellwork in order to ground yourself. Simply hold the stone while sipping, or hold it in your hand above the drink and imagine its vibration energizing your cocktail before serving.

Snow Moon Psychic

After a long day, it can be hard to declutter your mind of all the to-dos and worries in order to really be present for divination. This strong herbal cocktail is to be sipped before and during divination to help induce a trance. Specifically, the potent combination of anise, jasmine, and thyme provides a nice cleansing effect and heightens psychic powers. Enjoy under the psychic light of the February Snow Moon for more magic.

Energies: *Spirituality, Power, Psychic Abilities*

SERVES 1

2 tablespoons anise liqueur

1 jigger (1½ ounces) Jasmine Gin (see recipe in Chapter 4)

2 small fresh sprigs thyme, divided

2 tablespoons Jasmine-Cinnamon Honey Syrup (see recipe in Chapter 4)

2 tablespoons tonic water

Add a few ice cubes to a cocktail glass. Pour in anise liqueur and set aside. In a mixing glass, combine gin, a thyme sprig, and syrup. Muddle thyme while combining. Add ice to fill ¾ of the glass and stir swiftly for a few moments. Rinse the cocktail glass with anise liqueur, then discard liqueur and ice. Strain the cocktail into the glass, add tonic water and a few ice cubes, and garnish with remaining thyme sprig.

ADVANCED MAGIC

Lapis Lazuli

Lapis lazuli (connected to the third eye and throat chakras) helps further psychic development and clear communication. Hold this stone while sipping your cocktail to heighten its psychic powers and promote open and effective conversations.

The Prosperous Pumpkin

Pumpkin is entwined in the fall season, and for good reason! Pumpkins are powerful abundance assistants, representing feminine energy and the earth's bounty. Combined with the stimulating energies of nutmeg and cinnamon, and prosperity-associated bourbon, this dessert martini is perfect for fall money workings.

Energies: *Abundance, Healing, Money*

SERVES 1

1 tablespoon canned pumpkin puree
1½ tablespoons pure maple syrup
1 tablespoon half-and-half
⅛ teaspoon ground cinnamon
¼ teaspoon ground nutmeg, divided
1 jigger (1½ ounces) bourbon
1 small dollop whipped cream, for garnish

Place pumpkin, maple syrup, half-and-half, cinnamon, ⅛ teaspoon nutmeg, and bourbon in a cocktail shaker. Add ice and shake firmly to ensure the pumpkin puree is thoroughly mixed. As you do so, tune in to the stimulating energies of the spices, mixing with the pumpkin and cream, as all of the ingredients join together to activate abundance in your life. When the shaker is cold, strain the cocktail into a martini glass. Garnish with whipped cream and remaining nutmeg. As you sip, your nose will welcome the prosperous energies of the nutmeg.

ADVANCED MAGIC

Nine of Pentacles

The Nine of Pentacles is a card of wealth, abundance, and luxury. Paired with the bountiful, stimulating energies of this pumpkin cocktail, the Nine of Pentacles can help elevate visualization and manifestation. Gaze at the card as you shake your cocktail, imagining your life continuing to be more abundant as you journey into the winter months.

Dispelling Gin Gibson

When it comes to protection, a simple ritual can be better than one that is complicated and drawn out. Associated with Mars and the element of fire, onion is particularly great for protection and exorcism. It is believed to absorb negative energies when quartered, and even help with illness. Make use of the magical benefits of onion by pairing it with gin, which has the additional protective properties of juniper, as well as clarifying vodka. Garnish with extra cocktail onions if desired.

Energies: *Protection, Exorcism, Healing, Prophecy*

SERVES 1
1 tablespoon dry vermouth
2 ounces gin
1 cocktail onion

Place an ice cube in a martini glass, add vermouth, and set aside. In a separate mixing glass, add the remaining ingredients, followed by ice to fill ¾ of the glass. With a cocktail stirrer, stir gin swiftly by flicking your wrist and allowing the spoon to remain on the inside edge of the glass, guiding the ice along. Think about the protective aspects of the juniper essence in the glass, and say something along the lines of, "Juniper berry, grant me protection," if you wish. Close your eyes for a minute as you tune in to these magical energies. Rinse the martini glass with vermouth, then discard vermouth and ice. Once the outside of the mixing glass is slightly chilled, double strain the cocktail into the coated martini glass.

ADVANCED MAGIC

The Tower

One of the most infamous cards of the tarot, The Tower represents destruction. However, this destruction is usually positive, as it symbolizes cleansing away all the things no longer serving you. Reflect on this card as you sip your cocktail to enhance its clearing powers.

Oak Moon White Russian

The December Oak Moon invites energies of peace and strength, reminding you that at the coming of winter, the sun is reborn, and the days will grow longer once again. An invigorating, soothing update to the classic White Russian cocktail, this grounding coffee concoction will sweeten up your spirit in the long, dark nights ahead. Enjoy after a nice meal as a dessert cocktail, or sip as you attune to the energies of the December Oak Moon.

Energies: *Peace, Wisdom, Strength*

SERVES 1
4 tablespoons vodka
2 tablespoons coffee liqueur
4 dashes black walnut bitters
2 tablespoons half-and-half
1 tablespoon pure maple syrup

Add ingredients in a bucket glass filled with ice. Stir to mix, imagining the energies of the coffee liqueur and walnut inviting mental stimulation, inner strength, and wisdom.

ADVANCED MAGIC

The Moon

The Moon card of the tarot can suggest confusion, but it also symbolizes the fog that lifts when you listen to your inner guide. This card matches the energies of the December Oak Moon, reminding you that even in the dead of winter, a new light will emerge when you find peace within yourself. As you enjoy your cocktail, visualize the guiding light of the moon in the tarot card shining bright to clear away any deception, invigorating you with wisdom, clarity, and inner strength.

The Jasmine Archer

Nearing the end of autumn, as life falls away and everything around you becomes more and more barren, you are invited to journey inward and connect with your true self. Sagittarius season greets this movement into winter, provoking you with questions about philosophy, your beliefs, and your purpose in life. Jasmine and prosecco help you to make this connection to your soul. This cocktail is just the thing to prompt inner spiritual growth as well as new and exciting spiritual ideas.

Energies: *Spirituality, Purification, Inspiration*

SERVES 1

1 jigger (1½ ounces) Jasmine Gin (see recipe in Chapter 4)

2 tablespoons lemon juice

½ tablespoon dry curaçao

1 tablespoon Jasmine-Cinnamon Honey Syrup (see recipe in Chapter 4)

2 ounces prosecco

Add gin, lemon juice, curaçao, and syrup to a cocktail shaker. Add ice and shake lightly, imagining the outer layers of your perception of yourself, and any limiting beliefs or philosophies you may have, falling away with each shake. Envision a light glowing stronger within you as these layers are peeled back. Once the shaker is cold, double strain the concoction into a champagne flute or wine glass and top with prosecco, visualizing a new you bubbling up to the surface.

ADVANCED MAGIC

Sea Jasper

Open-minded, spiritual Sagittarius dares you to make great changes in your life and also see things from a more positive perspective. A stone of joy and cellular memory, sea jasper is a companion to your Jasmine Archer magic, allowing you to access thought patterns and challenge those that keep you from growing. Hold sea jasper as you sip your cocktail to help in this deep self-awareness and personal exploration.

CHAPTER 6

Winter Cocktails

As the flowers close up and life tucks itself in for a long hibernation— the fish beneath the frozen water, the mother bear in her hidden cave—so too does the witch turn within during the cold months of winter. Where autumn offers a time of transformation, the cocoon of winter is for introspection and planning. The sun traverses through the structured sign of Capricorn, imaginative Aquarius, and dreamy Pisces, inviting solid plans and innovative, spiritual approaches to the possibilities ahead.

The recipes in this chapter turn those wintery energies of creativity, planning, and fertility into enchantments that will fuel your schemes and prepare for a fruitful spring. Bless the New Year with The Witch's Offering, sip the Fire of Inspiration to induce new ideas, and clear away stagnant energy with the Imbolc Cleansing Lemon Drop. Sip away to sow seeds for a flourishing, magical future.

Awakening Yule Mule

Put some pep in your step during the winter revelries with this revitalizing twist on the popular Moscow Mule. Traditionally made with vodka, lime, simple syrup, and ginger beer, the addition of pomegranate, rosemary, and zesty Bergamot-Ginger Syrup takes this cocktail to an enchanted new level. Enjoy the stimulating and purifying energies of these seasonal fruits and herbs on the longest night of the year (Yule), by sitting down by candlelight with pen and paper to jot down new ideas and inspirations.

Energies: *Healing, Purification, Inspiration*

SERVES 1

7 pomegranate seeds, divided

1 thin slice fresh ginger

1 tablespoon Bergamot-Ginger Syrup (see recipe in Chapter 4)

1½ small fresh sprigs rosemary, divided

1 ounce lime juice

1 jigger (1½ ounces) vodka

2 ounces ginger beer

Add 4 pomegranate seeds, ginger, and syrup to a cocktail shaker. Shake, reflecting on the purifying, seasonal energy of the herbs infusing the syrup. Add ½ sprig rosemary, lime juice, and vodka. Add ice and visualize the stirring energy of new ideas as you shake thoroughly. Once the shaker is cold, strain the mixture into a copper mug filled with ice, and top with ginger beer. Garnish with remaining rosemary sprig and pomegranate seeds.

ADVANCED MAGIC

Two of Wands

The Two of Wands is a card of contemplation. It represents pausing in the midst of your journey to retreat, restore, and plan. Where do you want to go in life, and how can you get there? As you sip your cocktail and write about the rebirth of your spirit, pull out this card for inspiration.

The Witch's Offering

There's nothing like curling up with a cup of spiced hot cider in the midst of icy winter. Wassail is a traditional mulled cider that dates as far back as the Middle Ages, enjoyed around the time of the winter solstice to ensure a good apple harvest for the next year. Often, this practice includes singing in orchards and pouring part of the mulled cider onto the roots of a tree as an offering. Filled with warming winter spices and blessed by the loving, abundant, and purificatory energies of apple, ginger, cranberry, and orange, this version is just the thing to fill you with warmth and rejuvenation in the cold tide.

Energies: *Love, Abundance, Purification, Fertility*

SERVES 6

⅔ cup sliced red apple, divided
6 cups apple juice
½ cup pure honey
1 teaspoon ground ginger
½ cup fresh cranberries
5 small orange peels
2 cinnamon sticks
1 tablespoon whole allspice
4 small lemon peels
3 dried bay leaves

Cut 3 apple slices in half; set aside for garnish. In a large pot, pour apple juice, honey, remaining sliced apple, ginger, cranberries, orange peels, cinnamon sticks, allspice, lemon peels, and bay leaves. Simmer over medium-low heat about 40 minutes. Pour into mugs, garnish with reserved apple slice halves, and drink immediately.

ADVANCED MAGIC

Petrified Wood

During the winter solstice, the longest night of the year, the sun is "reborn." It is a time of renewal and of the hope that abundance is around the corner. To connect to the years of magic cast during this night, sip your cocktail outside while holding a piece of petrified wood. Petrified wood is a powerful energy conduit for connecting to ancestors, nature spirits, and past lives.

The Golden Ram

Capricorn greets the turn of winter, inviting you to plan, persevere, and pursue. It is time to get to work! With the powerful, abundant energies of cinnamon, vanilla, and nutmeg, this Capricorn-inspired twist on a hot buttered rum will motivate you to get moving and help ground you in practical ideas for success. It's time to take whatever innovations the solstice manifested and pursue them. Sip on this cocktail while creating a business plan for the new year, doing manifestation and money magic, or completing a new moon manifestation under the Capricorn new moon.

Energies: *Money, Love, Abundance*

SERVES 1

1 tablespoon butter, softened
⅛ teaspoon ground cinnamon
⅛ teaspoon ground nutmeg
⅛ teaspoon ground allspice
5 ounces hot water
2 ounces dark rum
1 tablespoon Vanilla Syrup (see recipe in Chapter 4)
½ tablespoon Honey Syrup (see recipe in Chapter 4)
1 cinnamon stick, for garnish

In a mug, add butter and spices, imagining blessings and abundance coming your way. Then add in hot water, rum, and syrups. Stir ingredients with the cinnamon stick, visualizing the powerful, activating energies of the spices and rum being awakened and invigorated. Drop in cinnamon stick as a garnish.

ADVANCED MAGIC

Malachite

To heighten the magical Capricorn energy of this potion, hold a malachite stone as you write your action plans for the new year or say a prayer between sips of your cocktail. Malachite is a stone of abundance and creativity. As a crystal ally, it can help take your creative ideas and ground them in physical action steps.

Restoring Chocolate Lux

There's no better way to warm up in the cold winter season and revitalize your spirit than with a rich hot cocoa. With loving milk and chocolate, hot cocoa is like a weighted blanket for your soul. The added Vanilla Syrup and spices in this version will nurture your spirit through potent goddess energy. Enjoy under the light of the January Wolf Moon to bond with family and friends, or sip alone as you reflect.

Energies: *Love, Luxury, Happiness*

SERVES 3

3½ cups whole milk

⅓ cup unsweetened cocoa powder

1 tablespoon semisweet chocolate chips

½ cup granulated sugar

⅛ teaspoon salt

1 ounce Vanilla Syrup (see recipe in Chapter 4)

In a small pot over medium heat, warm milk until hot, about 5 minutes. Add cocoa powder, chocolate chips, sugar, and salt. Stir together, reflecting on the loving, uplifting energies of chocolate and milk. Pour into a mug and add syrup. Stir.

ADVANCED MAGIC

Queen of Cups

The Queen of Cups depicts a compassionate, caring woman offering a cup. The cup represents emotions and emotional vulnerability. Before you drink this cocktail, look upon the Queen of Cups and imagine that the potion you are drinking is the cup in her outstretched hand. As you sip, feel her magical nurturing energy fill your body.

The Lovely Lady

When it comes to health and wellness, papaya packs quite a punch. Native to Central America, it has been used for centuries for a variety of wellness treatments and medicines. It assists digestion, elevates beauty, and has even been used as an aphrodisiac. Utilize these powers of wellness, love, and beauty in this papaya-inspired bellini. Paired with bubbly wine and soothing Hibiscus-Rose Honey Syrup, it's the perfect cocktail for a new moon or full moon bath to appreciate your own inner power. Sip away to cleanse your energy and turn that cold winter day into an opportunity for self-care. Garnish with a papaya wedge.

Energies: *Love, Beauty, Goddess Energy, Health*

SERVES 1

2 (1"-long) chunks fresh peeled papaya

1 tablespoon Hibiscus-Rose Honey Syrup (see recipe in Chapter 4)

½ tablespoon lemon juice

4 ounces sparkling white wine

2 drops rose water

In a mixing glass or cocktail shaker, muddle the papaya with the syrup. As you do so, think about all the energies of beauty and wellness being released. Add lemon juice and transfer the mixture to a white wine glass. Add a few ice cubes and top with wine and rose water. Stir, taking in the sweet scent of the concoction.

ADVANCED MAGIC

Rose Quartz

Rose quartz is all about loving yourself and recognizing the beauty within and around you. It invites peace, comfort, and gratefulness. As you enjoy your Lovely Lady cocktail, hold a piece of rose quartz to heighten its magic.

Fire of Inspiration

Shut in from the winter cold? It's time to invoke your inner child and get your creative witch juices flowing. Whether you are an artist or just looking to engage your inner sun through a fun activity, this warm beverage is just the remedy for you. The spiritual, psychic, and energizing powers of jasmine, cinnamon, lavender, and lemon in this cocktail will boost your work with stimulating new ideas and visions. Sip while brainstorming new spell ideas or developing your artisan skills.

Energies: *Creativity, Divine Inspiration, Friendship*

SERVES 1

½ tablespoon lemon juice

2 dashes lavender bitters

1½ tablespoons Jasmine-Cinnamon Honey Syrup (see recipe in Chapter 4)

1 jigger (1½ ounces) bourbon

1 jigger (1½ ounces) hot water

1 cinnamon stick, for garnish

1 small orange twist, for garnish

Pour lemon juice, bitters, and syrup into a mug. Stir ingredients clockwise while saying, "From a place of divinity comes to me new creativity." Visualize a door opening, with creative light pouring through. Add bourbon and hot water, and garnish with cinnamon stick and orange twist.

ADVANCED MAGIC

Page of Wands

The Page of Wands symbolizes a wealth of creative ideas. While these ideas may be somewhat immature or short term in nature, they provide initiatory, exciting sparks. To imbue this added energy into your cocktail, place the card nearby for visualization as you mix the ingredients or put it underneath your mug as you stir and pour in the hot water. Gaze at the stimulating nature of this card as you sip.

Grounding Highball

Need a bit of grounding after ritual? Or perhaps you're having a hard time waiting out the winter, finding yourself in a slump after the wealth of new ideas that Capricorn season offered. With grounding bourbon, stimulating ginger, and brightening bergamot, this magical twist on the classic highball will do just the trick! Revel in seasonal spices and help renew your energetic balance. Use this simple-to-make drink after spellwork to help reground yourself in the present and renew your energy field.

Energies: *Grounding, Stimulation, Endurance*

SERVES 1
1 thin slice fresh ginger
1 tablespoon Bergamot-Ginger Syrup
(see recipe in Chapter 4)
2 ounces Hazelnut-Chamomile
Bourbon (see recipe in Chapter 4)
4 ounces ginger ale

Place ginger slice and syrup in a highball glass. Muddle the ginger, visualizing its purifying, grounding energy spreading as you do so. Add ice to fill, and pour in bourbon and ginger ale.

ADVANCED MAGIC

Red Jasper

Red jasper is a stone of endurance. It is connected to the lower chakras (root, sacral, and solar plexus), making it helpful for strength and energy and also for emotional support when significant changes happen in one's life. Hold red jasper while sipping this cocktail to promote its stabilizing forces.

Cranberry Protection

Who doesn't enjoy the ease of a vodka cranberry? Utilizing the Cranberry Shrub recipe in Chapter 4, this seasonal, juicy libation is packed with layers of flavor and is simple to put together. Cranberries offer protection, while rosemary invites purification (further enhanced by clarifying vodka), making this cocktail a go-to for enhancing protection work, cleansing your spirit after a long day, or focusing your energy as you get to magic-making.

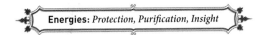

Energies: *Protection, Purification, Insight*

SERVES 1

1½ tablespoons Cranberry Shrub (see recipe in Chapter 4)

1 jigger (1½ ounces) vodka

1 ounce soda water

1 lime wedge, for garnish

Add shrub and vodka to a bucket glass. Toss in a few ice cubes, pour in soda water, and squeeze a bit of lime wedge into the glass before using as a garnish on the edge of the lip. Stir the ingredients, reveling in the deep red color and protective qualities of this simple concoction.

ADVANCED MAGIC

Nine of Wands

The Nine of Wands is a card of temporary withdrawal. It depicts the need to retreat before a final battle—to rest, prepare, and gather resources. Winter provides this exact opportunity, and when paired with the protective energy of cranberry, the magic of the Nine of Wands is magnified. Gaze at the Nine of Wands as you mix this cocktail, thinking of what information you need and what you may need to do to manifest your best self and best life in the spring. Stir the cocktail nine times to integrate the energy of the Nine of Wands.

Love Witch's Brew

Coffee grounds and beans have been used throughout history to divine the future, just as people read tea leaves. With the addition of cardamom, rose petals, cinnamon, and Vanilla Syrup, you have a lightly spiced, potent love spell to pass on to a lover, use for divining love, or just start your day energized and in a lovely mood—no matter how dreary the weather beyond your door may be. Make that coffee habit a part of your witchcraft! For a sweeter flavor, add cream to the finished drink before sipping.

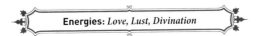

Energies: *Love, Lust, Divination*

SERVES 3

5 tablespoons ground coffee beans

½ teaspoon ground rose petals

¼ teaspoon ground cinnamon

½ teaspoon ground cardamom

2½ cups hot water

3 tablespoons Vanilla Syrup (see recipe in Chapter 4)

Mix ground coffee, rose petals, cinnamon, and cardamom together in a medium bowl. Trace an eye for psychic abilities into the mixture, then place your hands over the symbol and activate it with deep, intention-filled breaths, or by visualizing light channeling into the eye from your hands. Place the mixture in a French press and add hot water. Let sit for 3 minutes, then pour into a tempered glass or mug. Add syrup and stir.

ADVANCED MAGIC

Pink Calcite

Pink is a color of love and beginnings, and it can add a layer of loving magic to this divination potion. Utilize the vibration of this color and its power with pink calcite. Gaze upon this heart-opening stone as you mix your cocktail.

Mocha Persuasion

It can be hard to get active and productive in the cold winter, but this hot tequila drink is sure to get you moving. Inspired by the Mexican Mocha, it uses a blend of energizing cinnamon, vanilla, cayenne, and nutmeg to give you vitality, motivation, and energy. Use this cocktail to boost your power in any magical workings, when you need some motivation, or when you feel exhausted and just need to push through to the evening. Top with whipped cream for a luxe touch.

Energies: *Energy, Love, Money, Power*

SERVES 1

1 tablespoon semisweet chocolate chips

1 tablespoon heavy cream

1 tablespoon unsweetened cocoa powder

$\frac{1}{16}$ teaspoon cayenne pepper

$\frac{1}{4}$ teaspoon ground nutmeg

$\frac{1}{4}$ teaspoon ground cinnamon

4 ounces unflavored almond milk

4 ounces hot black coffee

1 teaspoon Vanilla Syrup (see recipe in Chapter 4)

1 ounce gold tequila

In a small pot over medium-low heat, melt chocolate chips with cream, about 10 minutes. Turn heat to low and let sit, stirring occasionally as you prepare the remaining ingredients. In a separate small bowl, mix cocoa powder, cayenne pepper, nutmeg, and cinnamon. Place your hands over the spices, take a centering breath, and imagine divine power flowing through your crown and down your arms and hands into the spices. Envision the energies of these herbal extracts glowing in response. Now add the spices to the cream and chocolate, then add almond milk, coffee, syrup, and tequila. Stir the concoction clockwise five times, feeling the increase of power in the mixture as you do so. Pour the cocktail into a mug. As you sip, visualize all of your grievances and boundaries breaking away. The road is open.

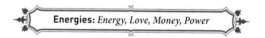

ADVANCED MAGIC

Carnelian

Carnelian is a powerful stone for energy and creativity. Its inspiration will invoke confidence and give you that extra energetic push. As you enjoy this mocha, hold a piece of carnelian, feeling the vitality rush through you with every sip. Then blow your intention into the stone, and place it in your pocket to keep with you as you go about your day.

Inner Child Sake

As winter begins to wind down, Aquarius season invites you to expand your imagination and your ideas about what is possible in the coming spring. Inspire the innovative, boundless energies of your inner child with this Shirley Temple-inspired sake cocktail. Your youthful self can show you new ways of doing things, how to solve some of life's problems, and how to have fun while pursuing your dreams. Attuned to the vibrations of creativity, childhood, and power through rice-based sake and ginger, Inner Child Sake will invoke your imagination. For added energy, spear the cherry with a lemon slice.

Energies: *Youth, Innovation, Imagination*

SERVES 1

3 ounces ginger ale

1 tablespoon Grenadine (see recipe in Chapter 4)

1 teaspoon lemon juice

1 ounce sake

1 maraschino cherry, for garnish

Add ginger ale to a collins glass. Top with Grenadine, lemon juice, and sake, and add ice to fill. Stir counterclockwise as though undoing any stagnant energy or stubborn thinking—slowly traveling back in time to childhood wonder. Top with cherry to remind you of the sweetness of life.

ADVANCED MAGIC

Six of Cups

Is your inner child hesitant to wake? Give the Aquarian energy of this cocktail extra potency by drawing a Six of Cups tarot card to reflect on as you sip. This card is one of nostalgia and innocence—making it a perfect enhancement when tapping into the joys of childhood. Gaze upon the card as though you were the child in the image receiving the cup—a cup representing unexpected gifts, pleasure, and limitless possibilities.

Fertility Hot Cider

As the days grow longer and spring peeks over the horizon, it's time to nurture the ideas birthed at winter solstice. Invoking the magic of the pentagram symbol (which combines fire, water, earth, air, and spirit), and the elevating and quickening energies of cinnamon, this fertility potion will protect and nurture your aspirations. Enjoy during the birth of the new moon, as it is from this phase that the moon will begin to grow. And as the moon grows, so does your wish.

Energies: *Fertility, Healing, Nurturing*

SERVES 1
4 ounces apple juice
1 small red apple
1 cinnamon stick
1 tablespoon Elderberry Honey Syrup (see recipe in Chapter 4)
1 ounce apple brandy
1 tablespoon spiced rum

In a small pot over medium heat, warm apple juice until it reaches a light boil, about 10 minutes. Meanwhile, cut a crosswise slice of apple so that the star-shaped pattern of the seeds is visible. Take a deep breath, and think about what energies you are trying to manifest. With this in mind, poke the cinnamon stick through the center of the pentagram of the apple slice, combining the quickening energies of cinnamon with the symbolism of the five spiritual elements. Imagine an energetic ripple effect as you do this. Drop the cinnamon stick and apple slice into a mug, and pour the syrup over them. Pour the heated apple juice into the mug over the cinnamon and apple, thinking about what you wish to receive. Add apple brandy and rum, and use the cinnamon stick to stir, saying a positive affirmation out loud as you mix your potion.

ADVANCED MAGIC

Ace of Pentacles

The Ace of Pentacles in tarot represents a budding opportunity blessed with success in the physical realm. Use the Ace of Pentacles to enhance the nurturing, supportive energies of your Fertility Hot Cider. Place the card under the cocktail while it steeps, and use it as a visualization tool as you craft the cocktail, imagining the five points of the ace of pentacles being contained with the five points of the apple garnish.

Imbolc Cleansing Lemon Drop

The halfway point between the winter solstice and the spring equinox, Imbolc celebrates the reawakening of the earth. Spring is coming, and it is a time to cleanse and prepare. What needs to be purified or cleared out from your life as you enter this period of renewal? This enchanted Lemon Drop celebrates the strong, citrus notes of Imbolc, with the additions of bay leaf and eucalyptus for more powerful cleansing. Drink as you do your spring cleaning, or as you bless seeds for new growth by your altar.

Energies: *Purification, Divination, Protection*

SERVES 1
1 jigger (1½ ounces) vodka
1 tablespoon triple sec
1 ounce Bay Leaf–Orange Syrup (see recipe in Chapter 4)
1 ounce lemon juice
2 dashes eucalyptus bitters

Place all ingredients in a cocktail shaker. Close your eyes while embracing the shaker, imagining the reawakening essence of spring and the cleansing and renewal it brings. Add ice, then shake and strain the beverage into a martini glass.

ADVANCED MAGIC

Jet

Jet has potent clearing and grounding energies that can enhance the cleansing magic of your lemony cocktail. As you sip, run a piece of jet through your aura, visualizing it capturing and filtering out all negativity expelled by the cocktail. Carry the Jet with you for protection and continued cleansing.

Love Divination Coffee

Irish Coffee is a popular dessert drink used to revitalize the mind and body after a heavy meal and counteract the effects of a sugar crash. Topped with whipped cream and ground nutmeg that greets the nose when sipped, this concoction is full of wholesome, loving, grounding magic. Perhaps you have a lover and want to do a bit of love divination on the relationship. Or maybe you want to balance the love with a little sensual lust. This Irish Coffee is perfect for heart- and body-warming spellwork on a chilly day when you're cuddled up inside with a loved one.

Energies: *Love, Lust, Grounding*

SERVES 1

3 ounces Love Witch's Brew (see recipe in this chapter)

1 ounce heavy cream

1 jigger (1½ ounces) Irish whiskey

1 teaspoon Vanilla Syrup (see recipe in Chapter 4)

1 dollop whipped cream, for garnish

⅛ teaspoon ground nutmeg, for garnish

Pour Love Witch's Brew, cream, whiskey, and syrup into a tempered glass mug. Place your hands above the mug, visualizing it glowing with a deep magenta light of love. Draw a heart in the air with your finger just above the mixture. Add whipped cream and nutmeg on top.

ADVANCED MAGIC

Morganite

Morganite is a stone that opens up the heart chakra—both to universal love and to wisdom from the divine and one's guides. Whether using your enchanted cocktail for love divination or to induce love, using this crystal can help open your heart. Hold the morganite in your hand while mixing, and keep it in your pocket or by your heart as you sip.

Money-Making Dark 'n' Stormy

Utilizing the prosperity herbs of ginger, bergamot, cinnamon, and mint, this refreshing Dark 'n' Stormy will invigorate any money-making magic. Combined with the fortunate energies of the March Seed Moon, this concoction is particularly useful in spellwork involving attracting clients and building a business. Enjoy under the light of the Seed Moon before lighting a green money candle, or while creating a business or career plan.

Energies: *Money, Power, Attraction*

SERVES 1

4 fresh mint leaves

1 jigger (1½ ounces) dark rum

1 ounce lime juice

1 tablespoon Bergamot-Ginger Syrup (see recipe in Chapter 4)

2½ ounces ginger beer

4 dashes Angostura bitters

⅛ teaspoon ground cinnamon

1 tablespoon ginger liqueur

1 small fresh sprig mint, for garnish

1 lime wedge, for garnish

Muddle mint leaves in a copper mug. Add rum, lime juice, syrup, and ginger beer. Top with bitters, cinnamon, and ginger liqueur. Stir the concoction, visualizing money and/or clients coming toward you. Garnish with a mint sprig and lime wedge.

ADVANCED MAGIC

Knight of Pentacles

The Knight of Pentacles can indicate persistence and payoff. All resources are available to him for long-term success. As you sip your cocktail, gaze upon this card, and imagine the cup you drink from is filled with abundance for the future.

Dreamwork Aviation Riff

After Aquarius season, Pisces flows in to invite relaxation and a focus on aligning with spiritual work. In order to be in alignment for this coming energetic growth in spring, it's time for some metaphysical upkeep. With ethereal jasmine, violet liqueur, and cherry liqueur, this twist on the classic Aviation cocktail is aligned to assist in dreamwork. And with an enchanting light-purple hue, what witch wouldn't enjoy this powerful libation? Garnish with jasmine flower and sip before deep meditation, or during magical workings to inspire dream exploration.

Energies: *Divination, Dreamwork, Luck*

SERVES 1

1 tablespoon violet liqueur

1 tablespoon maraschino liqueur

1 tablespoon lemon juice

1 jigger (1½ ounces) Jasmine Gin (see recipe in Chapter 4)

1 dash lavender bitters

In a mixing glass, pour violet liqueur, maraschino liqueur, lemon juice, Jasmine Gin, and lavender bitters. Add ice and stir, thinking of mystical Pisces energy as you do so. Trace the symbol for Pisces or Neptune into the beverage with a spoon to add extra energy. Transfer the drink to a coupe glass and enjoy.

ADVANCED MAGIC

Blue Apatite

Watery Pisces is all about diving deep into the subconscious and supernatural. To enhance the Piscean magic of this cocktail for even more potent dreamwork, place a blue apatite crystal on your forehead while you sleep after sipping the cocktail, or hold it in your hand as you drink prior to psychic divination work. This potent stone enhances psychic abilities and aids in accessing knowledge, making it a perfect ally to Pisces.

Uncrossing Mint Julep

Before jumping into the sensual, fertile energies of spring, it's a good idea to do a bit of energetic cleansing! With fresh peppermint leaves, Nettle-Hyssop Syrup, and a gin base to layer in the essence of cleansing and protective juniper, this Uncrossing Mint Julep is packed with strong purifying and protective energy.

Energies: *Purification, Exorcism, Protection*

SERVES 1

7 fresh peppermint leaves

1 tablespoon Nettle-Hyssop Syrup (see recipe in Chapter 4)

1 jigger (1½ ounces) gin

1 small fresh sprig mint, for garnish

1 lime wedge, for garnish

In a copper mug, muddle peppermint leaves in syrup. Imagine their combined, purifying energies being activated. Pour in gin and fill the rest of the mug with crushed ice. (Don't have access to crushed ice? Double-bag some ice cubes, wrap in a towel, and use a rolling pin or other blunt kitchen tool to pound it out—along with any negativity!) Stir the concoction counterclockwise, imagining unwanted energy being removed, and garnish with mint sprig and lime wedge to squeeze at will for extra hex-breaking potency.

ADVANCED MAGIC

Shungite

Shungite is a powerful stone for energetic cleansing and purification. While sipping your Uncrossing Mint Julep, hold a piece of shungite against the back of your neck to help remove negative energetic debris.

CHAPTER 7

Spring Cocktails

In spring, all life emerges from the hibernation of winter. While winter brought forth introspection, self-progress, and planning, the renewing energy of spring invites you to bounce back out into the outer world. It is a time of new beginnings, growth, and beauty. Spring brings forward ambitious Aries energy; stable, luxurious Taurus energy; and inspired, communicative Gemini energy.

The magical libations in this chapter turn these energies of spring—awakening and movement, lust and love—into sippable spells. You'll invoke new beginnings with The Bewitched Egg, imbibe a Seven-Herb Blessing to cleanse your spirit and manifest prosperity, and get focused on your goals with The Decider. Whatever you desire for this season of growth, the cocktails in this chapter will help bring those intentions into fruition.

Expedite Elixir

Sometimes you need something and need it fast! Utilize the energies of the patron saint of fast luck with this Saint Expedite cocktail. A spicy twist on the Old-Fashioned, this enchanted libation is powered by Saint Expedite's token herbs of cinnamon and rose, and elevated by the stimulating energies of ginger and abundant vanilla. Whether you wish to manifest money or a job, or get rid of obstacles, call upon Saint Expedite's aide with this cinnamony, sweet cocktail. (Just be sure to leave him an offering when your wish comes true!)

Energies: *Luck, Money, Quickening*

SERVES 1

¾ teaspoon Vanilla Syrup (see recipe in Chapter 4)

1½ tablespoons Goldschläger

1½ tablespoons Domaine de Canton

2 drops rose water

Pour all ingredients into a bucket glass. Carefully drop in one large ice cube. Stir the cocktail with the cube to allow the ingredients to mix. As you do so, bring your attention to the alchemical joining of the magical herbal spirits, and say: "Saint Expedite, come to my aid. Today, grant the wish I make."

ADVANCED MAGIC

Lodestone

Lodestone is a natural magnetized mineral. Known for its ability to attract, it is a perfect match for the energies of your Saint Expedite cocktail. To utilize the energies of lodestone within this potion, write what it is you desire on a small piece of paper. Anoint the corners and then the center of this paper with a small amount of the cocktail liquid. Fold the paper toward you, visualizing what you desire coming to you. Now place the lodestone on top of the paper, and drink the cocktail. When you have finished your magic work, place the lodestone and paper in a small pouch and keep it with you until your desire manifests.

The Bewitched Egg

The festival of Ostara ushers in the rekindling of life and the fertile earth of spring. Ostara is often celebrated with eggs and fresh flowers. Inspired by the clover club cocktail, this bewitched libation is a rejuvenating elixir with light floral notes. The tequila offers energies of youth and love, though you can use gin in its place to inspire more cleansing influences. Enjoy while celebrating the new vegetation around you or while working fertility and renewal rites.

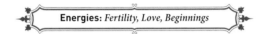

Energies: *Fertility, Love, Beginnings*

SERVES 1

1 ounce Elderberry Honey Syrup (see recipe in Chapter 4)
1 ounce lemon juice
½ tablespoon violet liqueur
¼ teaspoon rose water
1 small fresh sprig rosemary
2 ounces silver tequila
1 small egg white

Place syrup, lemon juice, violet liqueur, rose water, rosemary, and tequila in a cocktail shaker. Over two small bowls, crack the egg and separate the white from the yolk. As you do so, visualize what you are creating or hoping to create this spring season. Reflect on how most animal life comes from eggs, and how with this opening of the egg, the sun and spring are now reborn. Set yolk aside for another use and add egg white to the cocktail shaker. Place your hands around or over the concoction, visualizing the renewing energies of the alcohol, lemon, violet, and elder flavors. Think about your own energy being revived and growing with abundance. Close the cocktail shaker and shake without ice vigorously for a few moments. Then open and add a few ice cubes. Shake again and double strain into a stemmed wine glass.

◆→ ——— ADVANCED MAGIC ——— ←◆

Peridot

Peridot is a stone of growth, prosperity, and unconditional love. From the spring equinox forward, the days will officially be longer than the nights. So, this is a great time to focus on growth. Utilize the energy of peridot in this cocktail by holding it while you drink, thinking about what you want to grow in your life this season.

Sun and Smoke

Aries greets the start of spring with its fiery, intense energy. A stirring placement that motivates you to take charge of your life and follow your passion, Aries's forwardness is matched by none other than a spicy, invigorating ginger Margarita. The power and stimulating energy of ginger, aided by a dash of spicy cayenne pepper, is sure to get you moving into spring. Enjoy this magical cocktail while you set your goals under the Aries new moon, or at any time during Aries season when you need a bit of an energetic push.

Energies: *Energy, Power, Awakening*

SERVES 1

Celery salt, to rim glass

⅛ teaspoon cayenne pepper, plus extra to rim glass

1 jigger (1½ ounces) silver tequila

1 tablespoon ginger liqueur

1 ounce lime juice

1 tablespoon agave nectar

7 fresh parsley leaves

1 small flamed orange peel, for garnish

Rim a cocktail glass with celery salt and cayenne pepper. Set aside. Pour tequila, ginger liqueur, lime juice, and agave nectar into a cocktail shaker and add ice. Dash cayenne pepper into the shaker, visualizing the blazing-hot Aries energy falling into and stimulating the drink. Shake firmly and pour the cocktail into rimmed glass. Garnish with flamed orange peel to represent that Aries fire and excitement.

ADVANCED MAGIC

Ace of Wands

With the energy of Aries flaming through this Margarita, you are ready to set your intentions and manifest your desires. Enhance your Aries magic by drawing and focusing on the Ace of Wands tarot card while you craft your cocktail. The Ace of Wands is a card of inspiration and manifestation. Like spring, it represents the beginning of a new, fiery endeavor.

Flower Moon Harmonizer

The April Flower Moon is a time of beginnings, fertility, and growth. Spring abounds and life is blooming all around, but at night there is still calm as the light of the full moon graces the abundant green earth. Celebrate the floral, fertile, and gentle energies of the Flower Moon with this violet liqueur champagne cocktail. The peaceful energies of lavender and violet will invigorate you with hope, while the orange essence will inspire happiness. Sip on this bubbly cocktail to invite peace and harmony, or to aid in magical workings for growth and fertility under the light of the April moon. Substitute the orange peel for violet flower if you desire.

Energies: *Love, Peace, Purification, Harmony*

SERVES 1
1 sugar cube
1 small orange peel
1 dash lavender bitters
3 dashes Angostura bitters
1 teaspoon violet liqueur
3 ounces champagne

Place sugar cube and orange peel in a mixing glass. Drop bitters onto sugar cube and muddle, visualizing the fertile energies of the season awakening in this potion like a flower opening up in spring. Add violet liqueur and ice to fill, and stir with intention until combined. Strain the cocktail into a champagne flute and top with champagne. Twist the orange peel and add as a garnish.

ADVANCED MAGIC

Blue Sapphire

Blue sapphire is a stone of harmony and wisdom. Its soothing, peaceful energies invite healing and heighten psychic abilities and personal growth. The hue and energies of this crystal are a perfect complement to your Flower Moon Harmonizer potion. Hold the crystal in one hand as you craft the cocktail to help imbue the mixture with its energies, or to center yourself before drinking.

Seven-Herb Blessing

In hoodoo and conjure practices, a seven-herb blessing is a mixture that is boiled and added to a bath for cleansing, blessing, and abundance. Every practitioner's mixture is a little bit different. With the start of spring, why not enjoy an internal version of this potion for powerful cleansing and blessings? Utilizing several simple syrups and some green tea, this cocktail is easy to prepare and enjoy.

Energies: *Cleansing, Blessing*

SERVES 1

2 teaspoons Lavender-Chamomile Syrup (see recipe in Chapter 4)

2 teaspoons Nettle-Hyssop Syrup (see recipe in Chapter 4)

2 teaspoons Rosemary-Saffron Syrup (see recipe in Chapter 4)

1 jigger (1½ ounces) gin

3 ounces green tea, chilled or at room temperature

1 lemon wedge, for garnish

Place all three syrups in a collins glass. Add gin, and place your hand over the concoction. Close your eyes and imagine blessings coming your way with the renewal of spring. Add ice to fill, and pour in green tea. Lightly squeeze lemon wedge over glass, and drop into the cocktail. Stir clockwise briefly to bring new blessings into your life.

ADVANCED MAGIC

The World

The World card in the tarot symbolizes limitless possibilities and the completing of a cycle. In preparation for spring, this card can help you reflect on what you wish to bring into your life, and what needs to go. Place your hand over your finished cocktail while gazing upon this card. Visualize endless options for growth that the world has to offer buzzing within the mixed ingredients.

The Green Man

Amid the abundant growth of spring, it can be easy to feel overwhelmed and unsure of where to turn your attention. Harness the calming vibrations of lavender and beauty-inducing magic of cucumber with this enchanted take on the beloved Lemon Drop cocktail. With herbs and ingredients to soothe and transmute your energy, it is a delicious boost in peace and happy home workings.

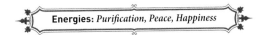

Energies: *Purification, Peace, Happiness*

SERVES 1

2 thin cucumber slices, divided

4 fresh mint leaves

1½ tablespoons Honey Syrup (see recipe in Chapter 4)

1 tablespoon lemon juice

1 jigger (1½ ounces) vodka

½ tablespoon orange liqueur

1 small fresh sprig lavender, for garnish

Place 1 cucumber slice, mint leaves, and syrup in a cocktail shaker. Muddle ingredients together, visualizing their cooling, soothing energies awakening and spreading in the shaker. Add lemon juice, vodka, orange liqueur, and ice; shake. Double strain into a coupe or martini glass, and garnish with remaining cucumber and lavender sprig.

ADVANCED MAGIC

Blue Calcite

Blue calcite is a calming, stress-reducing stone. To add this enhancement to your potion, hold the crystal against the cocktail glass, visualizing yourself calm and peaceful. Hold the stone in one hand while you drink the potion, then place it on your throat or forehead before lying down for a quick rest.

Love's Lucky Charm

What witch couldn't use a bit of good luck? Perhaps you are hoping to meet a new friend or want to invoke unexpected gifts. With the flavors of cherry, strawberry, and Grenadine, this tart cocktail brings fortune to your life and may also stimulate love as well. Sip this cocktail to strengthen luck rituals or as a good luck ritual itself, or bring it to an event to stimulate flirting and love. Garnish with a strawberry slice.

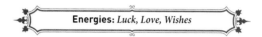

Energies: *Luck, Love, Wishes*

SERVES 1

3 thin slices fresh strawberry

2 fresh dark cherries, pitted

1½ tablespoons Simple Syrup (see recipe in Chapter 4)

1 jigger (1½ ounces) lemon juice

3 ounces ginger beer

1 ounce spiced rum

1 tablespoon bourbon

½ tablespoon Grenadine (see recipe in Chapter 4)

Place strawberry slices, cherries, syrup, and lemon juice in a collins glass. Muddle these ingredients together, thinking of their lucky energies mingling and growing. Say, "Cherries, sugar, and strawberries so sweet, give to me good luck on repeat" as you muddle. Now add ginger beer and a few ice cubes, then rum and bourbon. Top with Grenadine and stir clockwise as though moving the wheels of the universe in your favor.

ADVANCED MAGIC

Tigereye

Tigereye is known for assisting in matters of willpower and confidence, but it is also used for attracting good luck. To utilize this extra layer of magical energy, hold the crystal while prepping and sipping your cocktail, and blow your intention onto it. Keep it in your pocket for extra luck!

Paloma Potion

In need of an easy cleansing potion after a long day? This revitalizing version of a classic paloma uses a blend of cheering grapefruit and clarifying rosemary to magically lift your mood and recenter your mind. It is also perfect for tapping into a positive mindset before engaging in more solemn magic work.

Energies: *Purification, Mental Powers, Mood*

SERVES 1

1 jigger (1½ ounces) silver tequila

2¼ ounces grapefruit juice

⅛ teaspoon salt

1½ tablespoons Rosemary–Saffron Syrup (see recipe in Chapter 4)

½ tablespoon lime juice

2½ ounces soda water

1 small fresh sprig rosemary, for garnish

Add tequila, grapefruit juice, salt, and syrup to a collins glass. Add a few ice cubes, lime juice, and soda water. Stir counterclockwise to cleanse, then clockwise to inspire new, aligned energy. Garnish with rosemary sprig.

ADVANCED MAGIC

Blue Kyanite

Kyanite is associated with all seven chakras, and can rebalance and cleanse energy. More specifically, it helps to open the chakras and promote energy flow. As you drink this cocktail, hold a piece of blue kyanite in your hand or on the back of your neck to use its powers.

Venus Spritzer

After invigorating, stimulating Aries, we enter grounded, stable Taurus season. Ruled by the planet Venus, Taurus is a time of luxury, pleasure, and materialism. Inspired by Venus herself, this bewitching rosé vodka spritzer will invite harmony, beauty, and love into your life. Prepare extra servings for a gathering of your best witch friends, sip to delight in the luxurious pleasures of life under the Taurus new moon, or use in work involving abundance and gifts.
Garnish with extra lavender.

Energies: *Abundance, Luxury, Love*

SERVES 1
1 thin slice cucumber
4 fresh spearmint leaves
1 small fresh sprig lavender
1½ tablespoons Honey Syrup (see recipe in Chapter 4)
2 teaspoons lemon juice
2 ounces rosé vodka
1 jigger (1½ ounces) tonic water
1 small fresh sprig mint, for garnish

Place cucumber, spearmint, lavender, and syrup in a bucket glass. Take a moment to smell the refreshing, brightening energies of these herbs. Muddle them together, thinking about the sweetness and finer things in life they represent. Add lemon juice, vodka, and a few ice cubes. Top with tonic water and stir, thinking about the buzzing energies of spring and life. Garnish with mint sprig.

ADVANCED MAGIC

Grape Agate

Taurus loves to indulge in the pleasures of life, taking in all its beauty and fortune. To enhance the abundant magic of this Taurean cocktail, hold grape agate while sipping. Forming in the shapes of little grapes, this beautiful crystal embodies luxury.

Elderberry Healing Potion

Now is a key time to utilize the renewing energies of spring for healing work. With the cleansing juniper essence of gin and lemon, and healing elderberry honey, this concoction can assist in any healing magic. Rebalance your body with a few delicious sips.

Energies: *Healing, Protection, Purification*

SERVES 1

1 ounce lemon juice

1 ounce Elderberry Honey Syrup (see recipe in Chapter 4)

2 ounces soda water

1 ounce gin

Pour lemon juice and syrup into a collins glass. Add ice to fill, and top with soda water. With a spoon, stir the drink while saying an incantation and/or envisioning the healing, loving essence of the herbs infusing the mixture. Add gin.

— **ADVANCED MAGIC** —

Nephrite Jade

Nephrite jade is a powerful healer often used to increase the speed of the healing process. Associated with the heart chakra, it helps to open one to life's abundance and transmute any blockages to prosperity. Hold it while sipping your cocktail to enhance your healing work. You can also wear nephrite jade for good luck.

Good Mood Mimosa

Nothing says spring like a sharp, awakening mimosa. With uplifting orange and mood-elevating grapefruit, this enchanted twist on the morning favorite will help purify and chase any bad feelings away. Enjoy as a part of a detoxification ritual, to uplift and elevate your energy, for a magical Sunday brunch with friends, or in workings involving renewal and awakening.

Energies: *Purification, Beauty, Happiness*

SERVES 1
2 ounces orange juice
1 tablespoon grapefruit juice
3 ounces champagne
1 small grapefruit twist, for garnish

Pour orange juice and grapefruit juice into a champagne glass. Place your hands over the juices, closing your eyes and visualizing a bright light growing and radiating within. Top with champagne and garnish with grapefruit twist.

ADVANCED MAGIC

Smoky Quartz

Smoky quartz is a great stone to use for detoxifying energy and grounding. In conjunction with this cocktail, it can enhance purifying and mood-boosting energies. Simply hold it above your potion, with the natural point facing downward into the beverage. Imagine divine light flowing through the crystal down into your drink. If it's clean, you can also use the quartz to stir the mimosa before sipping.

Milk Moon Beautifier

Spring is a time of youth and beauty. And there's nothing better to capitalize on that energy than with moon-associated milk. The addition of youthful lavender and honey give this sweet, warm potion beauty-enhancing powers. Sip on the evening of the full May Milk Moon, or to manifest beauty and complement self-care rituals and glamor magic.

Energies: *Love, Beauty, Youth*

SERVES 1
1 tablespoon dried lavender flowers
¼ cup powdered milk
1 cup hot water
2 tablespoons pure honey
1 ounce spiced rum
1 tablespoon Kahlúa

Place lavender and powdered milk in a mug. Place your hands over the mug, visualizing the energy of the full moon shining powers of beauty on you from above. Pour in hot water, and stir in honey until it dissolves. Add rum and Kahlúa.

ADVANCED MAGIC

The Star

Beauty extends far deeper than surface appearance. And beyond simple blessings, The Star tarot card is a symbol of healing and personal growth. It shines a light on inner beauty, and encourages you to pursue more of what makes you your best, most radiant self. Gaze upon The Star as you sip your cocktail, visualizing the liquid enveloping your soul, healing and renewing it. As the negative and stagnant energies are washed away, reflect on the inner light that is no longer stifled.

Beltane Bee's Knees

An invigorating, fiery festival, Beltane welcomes the coming summer and celebrates fertility. It is an important day of sensuality and the cycle of life and death. What better way to celebrate the essence of Beltane than with a floral, spicy Bee's Knees cocktail? With a refreshing, balanced mixture of cleansing and rejuvenating gin and lemon, fiery cinnamon, and floral rose water, this enchanted libation is great to sip while enjoying the festivities of late spring. Garnish with a lemon twist for extra cleansing.

Energies: *Lust, Love, Purification*

SERVES 1

1 jigger (1½ ounces) gin
1 ounce lemon juice
1½ tablespoons Jasmine-Cinnamon Honey Syrup (see recipe in Chapter 4)
4 drops rose water

Place all ingredients in a cocktail shaker, conscious of the fiery, refreshing, and floral elements of Beltane that the ingredients bring to the cocktail. Add ice and shake. Double strain into a coupe glass or stemmed cocktail glass. If you are hoping to inspire love and lust, trace an imaginary flame in the air with your finger above the cocktail, anointing it with its passionate energy.

ADVANCED MAGIC

The Empress

The Empress tarot card symbolizes creation. Enhance the magical correspondences to nurturing and abundance by focusing on her fertile image as you prepare your cocktail.

Memory Mojito

Nothing says spring like a refreshing Mojito. Packed with mentally stimulating mint, this classic cocktail makes a great go-to for enhancing mental acuity. With the addition of rosemary, this vitalizing libation assists in communication, mental powers, and memory work. Enjoy while reading a witchcraft book to better memorize the insights held within its pages.

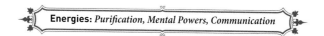

Energies: *Purification, Mental Powers, Communication*

SERVES 1
10 fresh mint leaves
1½ tablespoons Rosemary–Saffron Syrup (see recipe in Chapter 4)
1 ounce lime juice
1 jigger (1½ ounces) white rum
1 jigger (1½ ounces) soda water

Cup mint leaves in your hands. Take a deep, centering breath and imagine yourself of clear thought, focused, and easily able to retain information. Blow this intention onto the leaves, and visualize them glowing in response. Place mint in a collins glass and muddle with syrup. Add lime juice, rum, ice to fill, and soda. Stir clockwise, envisioning yourself retaining information as you study.

ADVANCED MAGIC

Fluorite

Fluorite is known as a focusing and mental acuity stone. As you drink your Memory Mojito, hold a piece of fluorite in your left hand, or place it on your third eye and visualize your ability to retain information expanding. Tune in to its soothing, mind-enhancing abilities.

The Wise Word

Gemini season opens the gateway from stirring spring to buzzing summer, with lots of communication, messages, and innovative ideas. Designed to utilize this astrological season, The Wise Word cocktail will help elevate and induce communication, provide new ideas, and enhance your thinking. Featuring refreshing lavender, purifying rosemary, and grounding walnut, it is the perfect potion to enjoy under the Gemini new moon.

Energies: *Communication, Innovation, Wisdom*

SERVES 1

1 jigger (1½ ounces) lavender vodka

2 dashes walnut bitters

1 tablespoon lemon juice

1½ tablespoons Rosemary–Saffron Syrup (see recipe in Chapter 4)

1 jigger (1½ ounces) soda water

Add vodka, bitters, lemon juice, and syrup to a collins glass. Add ice to fill, followed by soda water, and stir, visualizing the innovative ideas of these Gemini-associated herbs mixing together.

ADVANCED MAGIC

Blue Lace Agate

Airy Gemini is all about connection and the sharing of ideas, and you can enhance the energy of this zodiac sign even more by holding a blue lace agate crystal as you drink your enchanted cocktail. Associated with the throat chakra, blue lace agate is a powerful communication stone. It also can help soothe and calm energy, leading to wiser words and thoughts.

Aphrodite's Lust Potion

Take advantage of the sensual spring energies in true goddess fashion with Aphrodite's Lust Potion. Mixing sensual hibiscus, love-inducing lavender and rose, and honey to sweeten the soul, this eye-catching pink libation will have lusty lovers at your door. Sip to enhance magical workings, or serve to your desired lover. Garnish with a lemon twist.

Energies: *Love, Lust, Youth*

SERVES 1

1 ounce lemon juice

1 ounce Hibiscus–Rose Honey Syrup (see recipe in Chapter 4)

1 jigger (1½ ounces) silver tequila

1 ounce brut rosé

2 dashes lavender bitters

In a stemless wine glass, combine lemon juice, syrup, and tequila. Add a few ice cubes and top with rosé. Stir, dropping in bitters as you do, visualizing the lusty energy of the herbs coming to life and opening up like a red rose.

ADVANCED MAGIC

Knight of Wands

The Knight of Wands in tarot oozes with flirtatious, sensual energy. His fast-paced, fiery nature can heighten the power of your cocktail. Simply stir the cocktail atop this tarot card, being sure not to get it wet.

The Decider

While the stirring energies of spring are certainly exciting, sometimes the modern crafty witch feels overwhelmed. This grapefruit Gimlet is just the remedy! An alchemical mixture of the purifying energies of basil, rosemary, and grapefruit, it will help clear your mind and refocus on what is most important. You may also enjoy this potent cocktail in union with a guidance or clarity spell. Substitute the rosemary and grapefruit garnish for basil if preferred.

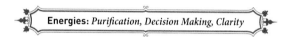

Energies: *Purification, Decision Making, Clarity*

SERVES 1

1 fresh basil leaf, torn

1½ tablespoons Rosemary–Saffron Syrup (see recipe in Chapter 4)

1 jigger (1½ ounces) vodka

1½ tablespoons grapefruit juice

½ tablespoon lime juice

1 small grapefruit peel, for garnish

1 small fresh sprig rosemary, for garnish

Add basil leaf and syrup to a cocktail shaker. Muddle together, visualizing the energies of the basil and rosemary fizzing together for mental clarity. Add vodka, grapefruit juice, lime juice, and ice. Shake firmly, and double strain into a coupe glass. Garnish with grapefruit peel and rosemary sprig.

ADVANCED MAGIC

Quartz

Quartz is the premier crystal for clarity of thought. This stone's energetic vibration will help clear your mind and tune you into your inner wisdom. Employ quartz's power in your cocktail by holding it in your hand as you sip, pondering what path to take.

Strawberry Moon Daiquiri

With hot summer days ahead, who wouldn't love a delicious, cool Strawberry Daiquiri? Attuned to the abundant, loving energy of the June Strawberry Moon, this cocktail is perfect for all relationship spells. The depth and sweetness of a dark rum complemented by love-inducing strawberries and uplifting lavender will help invite love, happiness, and abundance into your life. Specifically, you can use this potion to assist in magical workings related to opening your heart (or the heart of a partner or friend) to love and abundance. Try a strawberry garnish for added love.

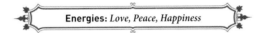

Energies: *Love, Peace, Happiness*

SERVES 1

1 medium fresh strawberry, hulled and sliced

1 teaspoon dried lavender flowers

4 drops rose water

1½ tablespoons Vanilla Syrup (see recipe in Chapter 4)

1 ounce lime juice

1 jigger (1½ ounces) dark rum

1 small lime peel, for garnish

Place strawberry slices, lavender, rose water, and syrup in a cocktail shaker. Muddle together, imagining their loving energies mixing together. Add lime juice, rum, and ice, and shake the cocktail hard, to make sure the strawberry flavor is expressed. Double strain the mixture into a coupe glass. Express lime peel over the glass, and then rim the glass with peel to get some extra lime essence. Twist peel and drop into the concoction as a garnish.

ADVANCED MAGIC

Ace of Cups

As the beginning of the Cups suit in the tarot, the Ace of Cups represents the beginning of emotions and opportunities. This card is all about opening the heart to love so that you are ready for what blessings may come your way. As you sip your cocktail, hold up this card and gaze upon it, imagining your cup is the Ace of Cups itself. Feel the strawberry, vanilla, and lavender inspire this expansion of love in your chest as you drink.

CHAPTER 8

Summer Cocktails

Summer is a time of growth, encouragement, and relationships. The seeds planted in early winter and spring are now in full bloom, with promise of success and harvest around the corner. The socializing solar energy of the season inspires outings and adventure, and love is affirmed and rejuvenated. In summer, we transit through nurturing Cancer, victorious Leo, and organized Virgo. Grains are plentiful, as well as many herbs such as basil, chamomile, lavender, mint, and elder. Strawberry fields grow full, and hazelnuts give their wisdom.

The recipes in this chapter utilize the social, thriving energies of summer to help you manifest the relationships and personal goals you seek. Sip on The Playful Fairy to connect with nature spirits, breathe new life into an existing relationship with Renewed Love, and invoke success in any endeavor with The Triumphant Lion. Through magical summer ingredients like sage, lavender, and chamomile, these cocktails are sure to bring enchantment to every part of the season.

The Playful Fairy

The summer solstice, known as Litha, is a time for fun, and the fae folk are out and about enjoying the weather. Pay homage to the fairies and their special day with this floral absinthe cocktail. A blend of herbs aligns the fae and their playful (and sometimes chaotic) energies, and this libation will help attune you to their ethereal vibration. Feel free to leave it on your altar as an offering to the fae folk, or connect to nature even more by creating a flower crown in the warm summer sun as you sip. You may even see a fairy!

Energies: *Purification, Fairies, Youth*

SERVES 1

½ tablespoon absinthe

1 ounce lemon juice

1½ tablespoons Elderberry Honey Syrup (see recipe in Chapter 4)

1 tablespoon violet liqueur

1½ tablespoons orange liqueur

1 ounce white rum

In a coupe glass, add a few ice cubes and absinthe. Set aside. In a cocktail shaker, add lemon juice, syrup, violet liqueur, orange liqueur, and rum. Shake the cocktail, and as you do so, be aware of how each herb is tied to and associated with the fae. Imagine their whimsical, menacing energies. Add ice and shake again until chilled. Complete an absinthe rinse in the coupe glass, then discard the absinthe and ice. Strain the cocktail into the glass.

ADVANCED MAGIC

Chiastolite

The intersecting lines of the chiastolite crystal represent the intersection of our world with the ethereal world of other beings like fairies. To strengthen your own connection to the youthful power of the fae, hold and consciously tune in to the energy of this stone while sipping your cocktail.

Revitalizing Tequila Sunrise

The days are growing warmer, and everything is in bloom. Reawaken your summer spirit and creativity with this easy and delicious enchantment. Blending the rejuvenating agave plant spirit of tequila, the brightness of lemon, and fresh, smile-inducing orange, this cocktail will put a pep in your step. Sip to inspire energy, vitality, and new ideas. Garnish with an orange slice if desired.

Energies: *Youth, Creativity, Purification*

SERVES 1

1 jigger (1½ ounces) silver tequila
4 ounces orange juice
1 tablespoon lemon juice
1 tablespoon Grenadine (see recipe in Chapter 4)

Add tequila to a bucket glass, and top with orange juice and lemon juice. Take a moment to smell the refreshing citrus scents. Slowly add Grenadine so that it trickles down to the bottom and creates a stunning visual effect. As you do, imagine new ideas and inspiration seeping into your own energy. Feel free to draw the symbol for the sun with your finger above the cocktail to give it even more revitalizing power.

— ADVANCED MAGIC —

Citrine

A solar plexus and sacral chakra stone, citrine re-energizes and inspires positivity and new ideas. To heighten the magic of your Revitalizing Tequila Sunrise, hold a citrine crystal in one hand while you mix the drink, and also as you sip it.

Lavender Sazerac

Attune your senses to the world of plant magic with the delicious blend of grounding whiskey, fairy-associated absinthe, and floral lavender and violet in this potent Lavender Sazerac. Enjoy as you tend to your witch's garden or to strengthen your connection with herbs as you practice any magic.

Energies: *Purification, Peace, Fairies, Spirituality*

SERVES 1

½ tablespoon absinthe
1 small sugar cube
2 dashes lavender bitters
2 dashes Angostura bitters
2 dashes Peychaud's bitters
½ tablespoon violet liqueur
1 jigger (1½ ounces) rye whiskey
1 small fresh sprig lavender,
for garnish

Add absinthe and an ice cube to a bucket glass and set aside. Add sugar cube and bitters to a mixing glass. Muddle together and add violet liqueur, whiskey, and ice to fill. Stir. Rinse highball glass with absinthe, then pour out rinse and strain cocktail into glass. Garnish with lavender sprig.

ADVANCED MAGIC

Green Kyanite

Green kyanite has a strong affinity with nature spirits and devas, and it can be used to connect with these spirits on a deeper level. These associations make green kyanite a great enhancement to your Sazerac cocktail. To imbue the beverage with this crystal, hold it in one hand as you mix your drink, then hold it above the glass once it's done, and while sipping.

Purifying Vodka Collins

After a long day, there's nothing quite like bathing in the cleansing smoke and scents of lavender and sage. Why not utilize these summer herbs in an internally purifying libation? Leave the stressful, heavy energies of the day behind and sip on this cocktail to cleanse your spirit and refresh your energy before engaging in ritual work, or to simply unwind. Garnish with fresh sage.

Energies: *Purification, Longevity, Peace*

SERVES 1

1 fresh sage leaf

1 ounce Lavender-Chamomile Syrup (see recipe in Chapter 4)

1 ounce lemon juice

1 jigger (1½ ounces) vodka

2 ounces soda water

Add sage leaf and syrup to a collins glass. Muddle these ingredients, imagining the cleansing aromas of the sage leaf being released and magnified by the sugars of the syrup. Add a few ice cubes, then add lemon juice, vodka, and soda water. Stir the cocktail counterclockwise, visualizing any negative energy being unwound and washed away.

ADVANCED MAGIC

Selenite

Selenite is a salt-based crystal, famed in the metaphysical and witchcraft communities for its purifying abilities. Able not only to extract negative energy but also to raise your vibration, this crystal is a perfect companion for your Purifying Vodka Collins. As you sip this libation before engaging in ritual and magical practices, run the selenite crystal through the air surrounding your body to help cleanse your aura and elevate energy for potent magic.

Spiritual Healing Elixir

In the middle of the hot and invigorating go-and-get-'em energies of summer, we encounter watery Cancer. Ruled by the Moon, Cancer can engage your emotional body and induce a desire to be a bit lazy. Every hard worker needs a break every now and then, and the sun in Cancer provides a key opportunity for self-care and healing in the midst of so much active energy. The Cancer-oriented herbal energies of this refreshing blackberry, hibiscus, and rose Mojito magnify the nurturing properties of the Cancer sun, helping you focus on what part of you needs care and attention right now. Top with speared blackberry.

Energies: *Healing, Love, Protection*

SERVES 1

1 large blackberry

1 large basil leaf

2 tablespoons Hibiscus-Rose Honey Syrup (see recipe in Chapter 4)

1 ounce lime juice

1 jigger (1½ ounces) white rum

1 ounce soda water

Place blackberry, basil leaf, and syrup in a collins glass. Muddle the ingredients together, imagining their nurturing, loving energy infusing and blessing the glass. Add a few ice cubes, and pour in lime juice, rum, and soda water. Stir the drink, connecting with watery Cancer as you do so. Feel free to draw the symbol of the Cancer sun sign in the air with your finger as you finish making the drink.

ADVANCED MAGIC

Chrysocolla

It is time to check in with yourself through the energies of Cancer. And your Cancerian cocktail can be enhanced even further by pairing it with chrysocolla, a nurturing, emotion-soothing stone. Connecting the heart and throat chakras, chrysocolla promotes deep emotional awareness and self-expression. Hold the chrysocolla stone in your left hand as you sip. In between sips, close your eyes and breathe deep into your belly. Notice how your body feels, and explore what it is saying.

Love's Last Word

A blend of purifying juniper-based gin, lime juice, aphrodisiac-associated green Chartreuse, and sweet cherry liqueur, Love's Last Word is a strong love potion. Infuse the gin with jasmine, and this cocktail becomes an elevated expression of soul love. Enjoy with a partner to honor your connection, or alone to inspire love in a fulfilling way. Top with black cherries for an eye-catching result.

Energies: *Spirituality, Love, Divination*

SERVES 1
1½ tablespoons lime juice
1½ tablespoons green Chartreuse
1½ tablespoons Jasmine Gin (see recipe in Chapter 4)
1 ounce maraschino liqueur

Pour lime juice, Chartreuse, gin, and maraschino liqueur into a cocktail shaker. Add ice and shake. Contemplate the alchemical mixing of ingredients as you prepare the drink, comparing this act with the alchemical mixing of souls. Double strain the potion into a chilled coupe glass. Draw a heart in the air with your finger above the glass.

ADVANCED MAGIC

The Lovers

The Lovers card in tarot represents attraction, beauty, harmony, love, and alignment. If using this cocktail to celebrate a loving partnership or to align yourself with your soul's true path, pull out The Lovers card as you mix the ingredients.

Spirited Summer Breeze

In the watery Cancer season, the July full moon is a time to tune in to your emotions, engage in some deep healing work, and clear the way for intuition connected to your heart. After all, your heart is one of the most intuitive parts of your body, and both the July moon and Cancer season remind you of the importance your heart plays in your spiritual life. Attuned to these spiritual, purpose-driven energies of the July moon, this cocktail can facilitate dreamwork, connection to one's spiritual purpose or spirit guides, and contemplation of karmic patterns that may need healing. Spear a lemon twist with whole anise for a stunning result.

Energies: *Prophetic Dreams, Spirituality, Healing*

SERVES 1

1 jigger (1½ ounces) Jasmine Gin (see recipe in Chapter 4)

1 tablespoon Grenadine (see recipe in Chapter 4)

1 ounce lemon juice

½ tablespoon anise liqueur

1 tablespoon Blackberry Shrub (see recipe in Chapter 4)

2 ounces soda water

Mix gin, Grenadine, lemon juice, anise liqueur, and shrub in a collins glass. Add crushed ice to fill and top with soda water. Stir the beverage, thinking of the watery energies of Neptune and the moon mixing to create a spiritual and dreamy libation. Drink outside in the light of the moon and contemplate your spiritual path.

ADVANCED MAGIC

Turquoise

Turquoise is a throat chakra crystal that inspires the communication of your spiritual wisdom. To enhance the spiritual, contemplative aspects of this cocktail, hold a piece of turquoise in one hand while you sip and gaze at the moon. Feel free to rest the stone on your forehead as you sleep to facilitate magical dreaming.

Celebratory Sangria

Summer is a time for play and community. Manifest great times with friends and family this season with this refreshing Celebratory Sangria. The playful, happy energy of oranges and love-invoking energy of raspberries and crabapples are sure to provide harmony, happiness, and abundance.

Energies: *Love, Happiness, Success*

SERVES 6

1 (750-milliliter) bottle pink moscato

2 ounces triple sec

2 ounces white rum

½ cup apple juice

¾ cup sliced fresh crabapples

¾ cup fresh raspberries

½ cup sliced hulled strawberries

2 thin slices fresh ginger

1 large orange, sliced

8 tablespoons Hibiscus-Rose Honey Syrup (see recipe in Chapter 4)

12 dashes lavender bitters

Place all ingredients except bitters in a large pitcher. Stir the mixture, thinking about everyone coming together as you do. Place your hands over the pitcher, close your eyes, and visualize happiness, communication, and harmony raining down like light from above you into the sangria. Store in the refrigerator for 2 hours before serving, up to overnight. Serve in stemless wine glasses.

ADVANCED MAGIC

Ten of Cups

The Ten of Cups in tarot is a card of harmony and celebration. Before mixing your elixir, pull out this card and think about the gathering you will be bringing the sangria to. Visualize everyone feeling happy and communicating in harmony and love with one another. Keep the card displayed while you stir the Sangria, and consider putting it in the refrigerator underneath the pitcher overnight.

Siren's Song

Nothing says summer like a Piña Colada. A pink take on this classic cocktail, the Siren's Song will lure you with her flavorful magic. This enchanted potion is sure to invoke some of the playfulness, creativity, and confidence of Leo season, and it also makes the perfect offering for the goddess of the seas herself. Enjoy on a hot summer day to cool down and invite some sensual play into your day.

Energies: *Love, Purification, Happiness*

SERVES 1

1 ounce Campari
1 ounce dark rum
2½ ounces pineapple juice
1 jigger (1½ ounces) cream of coconut
1 tablespoon orange juice
1½ ounces Hibiscus-Rose Honey Syrup (see recipe in Chapter 4)
2 dashes Angostura bitters
½ large frozen banana
1 tablespoon lime juice
1 small orange slice, for garnish
1 fresh pineapple leaf, for garnish

Add Campari, rum, pineapple juice, cream of coconut, orange juice, syrup, bitters, banana, and lime juice to a blender. Cover, then place your hands on either side of the blender, closing your eyes and imagining yourself inspired by this creative, joyful, sensuous energy. Once you feel the ingredients vibrate back with your visualization, add 1 cup of ice and blend until smooth. Pour the drink into a hurricane glass, breathing in the aromas and imagining your cup being filled with joy. Garnish with orange slice and pineapple leaf.

—→ **ADVANCED MAGIC** ←—

Honey Calcite

Honey calcite is a stone of creativity, sexuality, playfulness, and confidence. Inviting solar energy into your vibrational field, honey calcite manifests balance, joy, and hope. Its inspiring energy also urges you to take action and break old patterns and habits. To utilize the joyful, sensual energies of honey calcite, hold the stone while you sip your cocktail, then place it on your stomach or solar plexus chakra for a few moments once you have finished the drink.

Harmony Healer

Uniting the herbs of lavender and chamomile, and the fruits strawberry and lemon, this enchanted cocktail is attuned to the energies of happiness and harmony within friendships. Serve up a large batch at your next gathering or to help invoke forgiveness and elicit heartfelt conversation with a close friend.

Energies: *Friendship, Harmony, Happiness*

SERVES 1
Ground lavender, to rim glass
Granulated sugar, to rim glass
1 jigger (1½ ounces) strawberry brandy
1½ tablespoons lemon juice
1½ tablespoons triple sec
1½ tablespoons Lavender-Chamomile Syrup (see recipe in Chapter 4)
3 dashes lavender bitters
1 small lemon peel, for garnish

Rim a martini glass with ground lavender and sugar, then set aside. Add strawberry brandy, lemon juice, triple sec, syrup, and bitters to a cocktail shaker. Place your hands over the mixture, and close your eyes to imagine the harmonious energies of these ingredients growing in vibration and resonating together. Add ice and shake. Double strain into rimmed martini glass, and draw the symbol of a heart above the mixture with your finger or a spoon. Express the lemon peel above the drink to bless it with socializing energies, then drop it into the drink.

ADVANCED MAGIC

Three of Cups

The Three of Cups is a card of celebration and happiness in the support of close friends. Use this tarot card to help visualize cohesion and happiness as you attune the ingredients of this cocktail to your purpose.

The Triumphant Lion

Capitalize on the solar, vibrant energies of Leo with this sun-oriented success cocktail. Based on the beloved Old-Fashioned, this enchanted mixture celebrates the summer and promotes energies of success and strength. Utilize the herbal associations of bay leaf, orange, hazelnut, and chamomile to invite creativity and wisdom as you triumph over your fears and energy blockages and take charge of your life. Whether you wish to be promoted at work or ace an interview, this recipe will help channel the confidence and radiance of Leo to make you stand out and claim the day. Complement cherry garnish with flamed orange peel and add a whole bay leaf if desired.

Energies: *Success, Strength, Wisdom*

SERVES 1

1 small fresh bay leaf

1 tablespoon Bay Leaf–Orange Syrup (see recipe in Chapter 4)

1 small orange peel

2 dashes orange bitters

2 dashes Angostura bitters

2 ounces Hazelnut-Chamomile Bourbon (see recipe in Chapter 4)

1 maraschino cherry, for garnish

Place bay leaf, syrup, orange peel, orange bitters, and Angostura bitters in a rocks glass. Muddle the ingredients, visualizing the movement of muddling clearing away any obstacles or fear. Add one large ice cube, pour in bourbon, and stir. Draw the symbol of the Leo sun sign with your fingers above the beverage. Rub cherry around the inside of the glass in the bourbon, then drop it into the glass.

ADVANCED MAGIC

Strength

Represented by the mighty lion, Leo is a sign of strength. You can enhance this energy in your cocktail even further with the Strength card. Traditionally featuring a woman holding open a lion's mouth with her bare hands, this tarot card depicts the ease with which your magical libation will inspire success. Keep it below your glass as you muddle the ingredients, being sure to focus on it as a guide for your energetic intention and mindset.

Renewed Love

Rejuvenate your relationship with a partner—or yourself—with this twist on the screaming fuzzy navel. Mixing radiant orange and wise and loving peach, this cocktail brings happiness back into a relationship. Alluring rose and lavender invite the added energies of peace and love. Drink this magical elixir to invoke heartfelt communication, purification, and clarity to assist in reconciliation magic. Garnish with a lavender sprig.

Energies: *Love, Luck, Healing*

SERVES 1
1 ounce vodka
2 ounces orange juice
1 tablespoon peach schnapps
4 drops rose water
4 dashes lavender bitters

Pour vodka into a bucket glass. Add a few ice cubes, orange juice, peach schnapps, rose water, and bitters. Stir the cocktail clockwise, visualizing the relationship moving forward in the right direction, with the refreshing energies of peach, orange, lavender, and rose oiling the wheels.

ADVANCED MAGIC

Temperance

The Temperance card in tarot signifies balance, patience, and purpose, and it can also be a sign of rejuvenation. The symbolism of Temperance helps further attune the energies of your cocktail, especially if you're invoking divine help. Before you present this potion to your lover, make one for yourself and hold one cup in each hand. As you do so, gaze upon the Temperance card and imagine an angel or spirit reaching out through it. Envision that the two glasses of the card are the ones in your hands, and they will help provide balance and renewal in your relationship.
Then share the drink with your loved one.

Protected Prosperity

Lammas brings the first bounty of the harvest season. The ideas stimulated in spring and the hard work and inspiration of summer have at last led to the culmination of your efforts. Success is in sight as fields of grain stretch high into the sky, ready to be cut. And what better way to celebrate this grain harvest than with a whiskey drink? A fruity but fiery cocktail, the Protected Prosperity invites energies of abundance and protection. The seasonal blackberry manifests prosperity while protective blueberry, fiery ginger, and whiskey ensure grounded and protected money. Based on the whiskey smash, this cocktail is perfect for magic surrounding making and securing money. Garnish with blueberries and a lemon wedge.

Energies: *Money, Protection, Success*

SERVES 1
2 medium fresh blackberries
4 medium fresh blueberries
1 jigger (1½ ounces) bourbon
1 tablespoon ginger liqueur
1½ tablespoons lemon juice
1 tablespoon Bergamot–Ginger Syrup
(see recipe in Chapter 4)
1 jigger (1½ ounces) ginger beer

Place blackberries, blueberries, bourbon, ginger liqueur, lemon juice, and syrup in a cocktail shaker. Place your hands on either side of the shaker, visualizing the desired effects of the cocktail. Are you seeking more protection? More abundance? Or perhaps protected abundance? Take a moment to tune in to those intentions. Once you feel the ingredients buzzing, add ice and shake. Pour the concoction into a bucket glass, and top with ginger beer.

ADVANCED MAGIC

Four of Pentacles

The Four of Pentacles in tarot represents financial security and saving money. It can also mean control and conservatism. The Four of Pentacles is a perfect correspondence to enhance the prosperous energy of your cocktail, so that you not only enjoy your money but also conserve it. Keep the card beneath your glass as you add the ingredients.

The Blockage Buster

Do you keep encountering delays? Or perhaps just feeling stuck? Clear the way and invite new opportunities with this blockage-busting twist on the Whiskey Sour. Lemon, rosemary, and lavender are traditional cleansing herbs, while walnut and hazelnut invite wisdom. The additional cinnamon and saffron invoke the sun's blessing and opening energies. It is a perfect libation to enjoy before any manifestation magic, to help open the way and provide wisdom before you work, or to sip away life's unsavory delays.

Energies: *Purification, Opportunities, Success*

SERVES 1

1 jigger (1½ ounces) Hazelnut-Chamomile Bourbon (see recipe in Chapter 4)

1 tablespoon lemon juice

1 tablespoon orange juice

1 tablespoon Rosemary-Saffron Syrup (see recipe in Chapter 4)

⅛ teaspoon ground cinnamon

2 dashes lavender bitters

1 drop black walnut bitters

1 small egg white

Place all ingredients in a cocktail shaker. Shake briefly without ice, then add ice and shake again until chilled. As you shake, imagine any blockages falling away and the radiance of the sun's light glowing from within. Strain the cocktail into a coupe glass. As you pour, visualize the golden mixture shining with the sun's radiance to fill your cup with energy and new opportunities.

ADVANCED MAGIC

The Sun

The Sun card in tarot symbolizes blessings, good communication, freedom, and positivity. It symbolizes that all is good for you to proceed. To utilize the energies of The Sun, keep this tarot card nearby as you mix your magical cocktail. As you sip, gaze upon the card to connect to The Sun–oriented ingredients, manifesting purification, energy, and vitality.

Barley Moon Shandy

Celebrate the start of the harvest season with a refreshing beer cocktail. Attuned to the August Corn/Barley Moon and the purifying flavors of lavender, chamomile, and lemon, this enchanted shandy will cleanse your spirit and awaken your third eye chakra. The grains of the beer and bourbon will also help ground you in ancestral and karmic wisdom. A cocktail of balance, this blend will support thoughts of balance in your own circumstances. What is ready to be harvested in your life? What do you still have to pursue? Enjoy under the purifying light of the August full moon.

Energies: *Abundance, Grounding, Psychic Powers*

SERVES 1

1½ tablespoons Lavender-Chamomile Syrup (see recipe in Chapter 4)

1½ tablespoons lemon juice

1 ounce bourbon

4 ounces pilsner

1 lemon wheel, for garnish

1 small fresh sprig lavender, for garnish

Place syrup, lemon juice, and bourbon in a cocktail shaker. Add ice, and shake. Strain into a pint glass, and top with pilsner. Spear the lemon wheel with the lavender sprig and use as a garnish.

ADVANCED MAGIC

Ten of Pentacles

The Ten of Pentacles in tarot represents abundance, stability, and contentment with all that one has built and created in life. This card is a great visual tool for enhancing the ideas of abundance and completeness in your Barley Moon Shandy. Gaze upon it while preparing your potion, imagining as you strain the cocktail that abundance is raining into your glass.

Mercurial Grounding Elixir

Following the fiery inspiration and vitality of the height of summer comes Virgo. Wrapping up the season and moving the earth toward fall, Virgo invites organization, perfection, and execution, and it's all about planning ahead. Whether you are seeking to ground and organize your thoughts, need a gentle refreshing beverage after a magic ritual, or want something to counter the blocking effects of Mercury Retrograde, this Virgo-inspired cocktail has your back. Blending the cleansing and purifying essence of juniper-based gin with the powerful herbal trio of chamomile, lavender, and mint, it will ground your energy and clear out the mental clutter.

Energies: *Purification, Grounding, Mental Powers*

SERVES 1

5 fresh mint leaves

1½ tablespoons Lavender-Chamomile Syrup (see recipe in Chapter 4)

1 ounce lemon juice

1 jigger (1½ ounces) gin

2 ounces tonic water

1 small fresh sprig mint, for garnish

Muddle mint leaves with syrup in a rocks glass. As you do so, imagine any and all mental clutter deteriorating. Add lemon juice, gin, tonic water, and ice to fill. Stir and garnish with mint sprig.

ADVANCED MAGIC

Hematite

Whether using this cocktail to ground and center during Mercury Retrograde, or to actively connect to the earthy and practical energy of Virgo, hematite is a great enhancement for your magic. A root chakra stone, hematite will repel negativity, sooth your own energy, and connect you to the earth's core. Hold hematite and tune in to its energy while enjoying your libation to invite more practicality and groundedness.

Wine Moon Cocktail

What better way to celebrate the September Wine Moon than with a red wine cocktail? The Wine Moon marks the entrance into the colder, waning months of the year. Attentions now turn inward to the home, making sure your space is ready and warm for the coming winter. Attuned to the Wine Moon and its energy, this juicy, grounding cocktail invites spirituality, wisdom, longevity, and abundance. So dust off that mantel and sip this warm harvest cocktail to invite introspection and spiritual wisdom, or enjoy as you cuddle up under the covers with a movie.

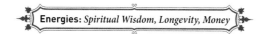

Energies: *Spiritual Wisdom, Longevity, Money*

SERVES 1

1 jigger (1½ ounces) apple brandy
3 whole cloves
1 ounce lemon juice
2 dashes Angostura bitters
1½ tablespoons pure maple syrup
3½ ounces medium-bodied red wine
1 small orange twist, for garnish

Place brandy, cloves, lemon juice, bitters, and maple syrup in a cocktail shaker. Add ice and shake. Pour into a red wine glass and add wine. Stir the concoction clockwise, visualizing the turning of the seasons, and the introspection and wisdom that come with it. Place your hands over the finished drink, closing your eyes and imbuing the beverage with wisdom and the abundance of life. Garnish with orange twist.

ADVANCED MAGIC

The Hermit

As the season changes from summer to fall, introspection begins. Guiding lantern in hand, The Hermit in tarot traverses the depths of his soul to reorganize his priorities and realign himself with his soul's true path. To heighten the elements of spiritual wisdom within your Wine Moon Cocktail, stir the finished concoction above this card. As you take your first sip, look upon the card and focus on the light of The Hermit's lantern to reawaken your own inner light.

Love Potion No. 10

Packed with potent love herbs and fruits, this cider will help take your love for someone special to the next level. Heart-opening basil and strawberry invoke happiness and blend perfectly with the loving energies of vanilla and apple to inspire devotion and commitment. Pair this cocktail with any love magic using complementary herbs, and enjoy with your partner to help deepen your relationship—or sip before and after performing a love ritual together.

Energies: *Love, Divination*

SERVES 1

2 large fresh strawberries, hulled and sliced

1 large fresh basil leaf

1 tablespoon Vanilla Syrup (see recipe in Chapter 4)

2 tablespoons lemon juice

2 ounces vodka

3 tablespoons apple juice

Muddle strawberry and basil with syrup in a cocktail shaker. Visualize your two hearts opening and melding together as you do so. Add lemon juice and vodka, and shake. Double strain into a coupe glass, and add apple juice.

ADVANCED MAGIC

Two of Cups

The Two of Cups in tarot is a card of spiritual union and divine love. Whether it represents the spiritual union of one with their own soul purpose, or the spiritual union with another person, it is a powerful card of intense connection. It can often also symbolize a new and balanced loving relationship. To imbue this love potion with the extra power of the Two of Cups, focus on the card as you muddle the ingredients and draw the symbol of the heart in the air with your finger above the cocktail glass.

Classic Cocktail Recipes

Once you practice mixing the different enchanted cocktails in this book, you can try putting your own unique twists on your drinks to focus their power on any intention or desired outcome of your choice. Of course, with so many herbs, alcohols, syrups, and more to choose from, you may be wondering where to even begin. The following section provides recipes for a number of classic cocktails. Use these time-tested, easy-to-follow favorites as a base for your creations. Then, add any edible elements you wish and begin your spellwork!

Americano

SERVES 1
2 ounces Campari
1 ounce sweet vermouth
Club soda to fill
1 orange half wheel, for garnish

Add all ingredients except club soda and orange to bucket glass and stir. Add club soda, then garnish with orange half wheel.

Apple Martini

SERVES 1
1 jigger (1½ ounces) vodka
1 tablespoon apple schnapps
1½ tablespoons lime juice
½ tablespoon Simple Syrup (see recipe in Chapter 4)

Add vodka, apple schnapps, lime juice, and syrup to a cocktail shaker. Add ice and shake until chilled. Double strain into a martini glass.

Aviation

SERVES 1
1 tablespoon maraschino liqueur
1 jigger (1½ ounces) gin
1 tablespoon lemon juice
½ tablespoon violet liqueur
1 maraschino cherry, for garnish

Shake all ingredients except cherry in a cocktail shaker, then double strain into a coupe or martini glass. Garnish with cherry.

Bloody Mary

SERVES 1

3 ounces tomato juice
1 jigger (1½ ounces) vodka
1 tablespoon lemon juice
⅛ teaspoon Worcestershire sauce
⅛ teaspoon celery salt
⅛ teaspoon ground black pepper
⅛ teaspoon hot pepper sauce
¼ teaspoon finely grated horseradish
1 large stalk celery, for garnish

Add tomato juice, vodka, lemon juice, Worcestershire sauce, celery salt, black pepper, hot pepper sauce, and horseradish to a cocktail shaker. Add ice and shake. Pour into a collins glass and garnish with celery.

Boulevardier

SERVES 1

1 ounce rye whiskey
1 ounce Campari
1 ounce sweet vermouth
1 small orange peel, for garnish

Place all ingredients except orange peel into a mixing glass, add ice to fill, and stir. Strain into a rocks glass over a few ice cubes. Express orange peel over glass, then drop in.

Caipirinha

SERVES 1
6 lime wedges
½ tablespoon Simple Syrup (see recipe in Chapter 4)
2 ounces cachaça
Soda water to fill
1 lime wheel, for garnish

In an old-fashioned glass, muddle lime in syrup. Fill the glass with ice, then pour in cachaça, followed by soda water to fill. Stir, and garnish with lime wheel.

Corpse Reviver No. 2

SERVES 1
1 ice cube
½ tablespoon absinthe
1 jigger (1½ ounces) gin
1 ounce Cocchi Americano
1 ounce lemon juice
1 tablespoon dry curaçao
1 maraschino cherry, for garnish

Rinse a coupe glass with ice cube and absinthe. Add all other ingredients except cherry to a cocktail shaker, add ice, and shake. Double strain into rinsed coupe glass and garnish with cherry.

Cosmopolitan

SERVES 1
2 ounces vodka
⅛ teaspoon cranberry juice
1 tablespoon lime juice
1 tablespoon dry curaçao
½ tablespoon Simple Syrup (see recipe in Chapter 4)
1 lime wheel, for garnish

Shake all ingredients except lime wheel in a cocktail shaker, then double strain into a martini or coupe glass. Garnish with lime wheel.

Daiquiri

SERVES 1
1 jigger (1½ ounces) light rum
1 tablespoon Simple Syrup (see recipe in Chapter 4)
1 ounce lime juice
1 lime wheel, for garnish

Shake all ingredients except lime wheel in a cocktail shaker and strain into a coupe glass. Garnish with lime wheel.

Dark 'n' Stormy

SERVES 1
2 ounces dark rum
1½ tablespoons lime juice
½ tablespoon ginger syrup
4 dashes Angostura bitters
Ginger beer to fill
1 lime wheel, for garnish

Add all ingredients except ginger beer and lime wheel to a rocks glass, then top with ginger beer and garnish with lime wheel.

French 75

SERVES 1
2 ounces gin
1 ounce lemon juice
½ tablespoon dry curaçao
½ tablespoon Simple Syrup (see recipe in Chapter 4)
Prosecco to fill
1 lemon wheel, for garnish

Shake all ingredients except prosecco and lemon wheel in a cocktail shaker, then double strain into a champagne glass. Top with prosecco, then garnish with lemon wheel.

Gimlet

2 ounces gin
¾ ounce lime juice
½ ounce Simple Syrup (see recipe in Chapter 4)

Add gin, lime juice, and syrup to a cocktail shaker and add ice. Shake until chilled, then double strain into a coupe glass.

Greyhound

SERVES 1
2 ounces vodka
4 ounces grapefruit juice
1 lemon or lime wedge, for garnish

In a rocks glass, add vodka then ice to fill. Pour in grapefruit juice, stir, and garnish with lime wedge.

Hemingway Daiquiri

SERVES 1
2 ounces white rum
1½ tablespoons key lime juice
1 tablespoon grapefruit juice
1 tablespoon maraschino liqueur
2 tablespoons Simple Syrup (see recipe in Chapter 4)

Add rum, lime juice, grapefruit juice, maraschino liqueur, and syrup to a cocktail shaker. Add ice and shake until chilled. Double strain into a coupe glass.

Hurricane

SERVES 1

2 ounces white rum

2 ounces dark rum

2 ounces passion fruit juice

1 ounce orange juice

Juice of ½ small lime

2 tablespoons Simple Syrup (see recipe in Chapter 4)

1 tablespoon Grenadine (see recipe in Chapter 4)

1 orange slice, for garnish

1 maraschino cherry, for garnish

Add a few ice cubes to a hurricane glass. Add remaining ingredients except cherry, stir, and garnish with cherry.

Last Word

SERVES 1

1 ounce gin

1 ounce green Chartreuse

1 ounce lime juice

½ tablespoon maraschino liqueur

1 small lime peel, for garnish

Shake all ingredients except lime peel in a cocktail shaker, then double strain into a coupe glass. Garnish with lime peel.

Lemon Drop

SERVES 1

Granulated sugar, to rim glass

2 ounces vodka

1½ tablespoons lemon juice

1 tablespoon Simple Syrup (see recipe in Chapter 4)

1 lemon wheel, for garnish

Rim a martini or coupe glass with sugar. Set aside. Shake all remaining ingredients except lemon wheel in a cocktail shaker with ice, then double strain into rimmed coupe glass. Garnish with lemon wheel.

Mai Tai

SERVES 1

2 ounces white rum

1 ounce lime juice

1½ tablespoons orange juice

1 tablespoon orgeat syrup

½ tablespoon dry curaçao

1½ tablespoons dark rum

4 dashes Angostura bitters

1 small fresh sprig mint, for garnish

1 orange wheel, for garnish

Place rum, lime juice, orange juice, and orgeat syrup in a cocktail shaker. Shake, then double strain over crushed ice in an old-fashioned glass. Float dark rum and bitters on top, then garnish with mint sprig and orange wheel.

Manhattan

2 ounces bourbon or whiskey
1 ounce sweet vermouth
2 dashes Angostura bitters
1 brandied cherry, for garnish

Stir all ingredients except cherry in a mixing glass. Double strain into a martini glass and garnish with cherry.

Margarita

SERVES 1
1 jigger (1½ ounces) silver tequila
1 tablespoon orange liqueur
1½ tablespoons lime juice
1 tablespoon agave nectar

Add a few ice cubes to a margarita glass. Add remaining ingredients to the glass.

Martini

SERVES 1
2 ounces vodka or gin
1 tablespoon dry vermouth
1 olive or lemon twist, for garnish

If using vodka, shake with vermouth and ice in a cocktail shaker and double strain into a cocktail glass. If using gin, stir ingredients in glass. Garnish with olive or lemon twist. To make a dry Martini, lessen the amount of vermouth or do a simple rinse. To make an extra dry Martini, leave out all vermouth.

Mint Julep

SERVES 1
4 fresh mint leaves
1 teaspoon confectioners' sugar
2 teaspoons water
2 ounces bourbon
1 small fresh sprig mint, for garnish

Muddle mint leaves, sugar, and water in copper mug. Fill the mug with cracked ice, then add bourbon and stir until the glass is frosted. Garnish with mint sprig.

Mojito

SERVES 1
6 fresh mint leaves
1½ tablespoons Simple Syrup (see recipe in Chapter 4)
1 jigger (1½ ounces) white rum
1 ounce lime juice
Soda water to fill
1 small fresh sprig mint, for garnish
1 lime wedge, for garnish

Muddle mint in the syrup in the bottom of a collins glass. Add a few ice cubes, then pour in rum, lime juice, and soda water. Garnish with mint sprig and lime wedge.

Moscow Mule

SERVES 1
2 slices fresh ginger
1 tablespoon ginger syrup
1 jigger (1½ ounces) vodka
1 ounce lime juice
Ginger beer to fill

In a copper glass, muddle ginger in ginger syrup. Add a few ice cubes and pour in vodka and lime juice. Top with ginger beer. Stir.

Negroni

SERVES 1
1 ounce gin
1 ounce Campari
1 ounce sweet vermouth
1 small orange peel, for garnish

Stir all ingredients except orange peel in a mixing glass filled with ice. Strain into an old-fashioned glass, add one large ice cube, and garnish with orange peel.

Old-Fashioned

SERVES 1
1 small lemon peel
1 small orange peel
2 dashes Angostura bitters
1 tablespoon Simple Syrup (see recipe in Chapter 4)
2 ounces bourbon
1 maraschino cherry, for garnish

Muddle lemon peel and orange peel with Angostura bitters and syrup in the bottom of an old-fashioned glass. Add one large ice cube, pour in bourbon, stir, and garnish with cherry.

Piña Colada

SERVES 1
3 ounces pineapple juice
1 ounce white rum
1 ounce coconut cream

Shake all ingredients with crushed ice in a cocktail shaker until smooth. Pour into a hurricane glass.

Screwdriver

SERVES 1

1 jigger (1½ ounces) vodka

6 ounces orange juice

Place a few ice cubes in a rocks glass. Pour in vodka and orange juice. Stir.

Sea Breeze

SERVES 1

3½ tablespoons vodka

3 ounces cranberry juice

1 ounce grapefruit juice

1 slice grapefruit, for garnish

Place a few ice cubes in a rocks glass. Pour in vodka, cranberry juice, and grapefruit juice. Stir and garnish with grapefruit slice.

Sex on the Beach

SERVES 1

2 ounces vodka

1 ounce peach schnapps

2 ounces grapefruit juice or orange juice

2 ounces cranberry juice

1 teaspoon lemon juice

Place a few ice cubes in a rocks glass. Add all ingredients. Stir.

Tom Collins

SERVES 1
1 jigger (1½ ounces) gin
1 ounce lemon juice
1 tablespoon Simple Syrup (see recipe in Chapter 4)
Club soda to fill
1 maraschino cherry, for garnish
1 lemon slice, for garnish

Place a few ice cubes in a collins glass. Add gin, lemon juice, syrup, and club soda. Garnish with cherry and lemon slice.

Vodka/Gin and Tonic

SERVES 1
2 ounces vodka or gin
1 tablespoon tonic syrup
Soda water to fill

Add vodka or gin and syrup to bucket glass. Top with soda water. Stir.

Whiskey Sour

SERVES 1
1 ounce lemon juice
1 tablespoon Simple Syrup (see recipe in Chapter 4)
1 small egg white
1 jigger (1½ ounces) bourbon

Add all ingredients to a cocktail shaker. Shake without ice first, then re-shake with ice until chilled. Double strain into a coupe glass.

White Russian

SERVES 1
2 ounces vodka
1½ tablespoons coffee liqueur
Whole milk to fill

Place a few ice cubes in an old-fashioned glass. Add vodka and coffee liqueur. Top with whole milk. Stir.

APPENDIX B

Herbal Intentions

✣ Abundance

Cherry

Clove

Cranberry

Maple

Orange

Pumpkin

Tomato

Vanilla

✣ Attraction

Apricot

Maple

Lavender

✣ Banishing

Basil

Chili Pepper

Clove

Coffee

Elder

Lime

Peach (*banishment through the manifestation of love*)

Nettle

Onion

Rosemary

✣ Beauty

Agave

Cucumber

Milk

Orange Blossom

Papaya

Peach

✣ Communication

Chamomile

Peppermint

✣ Creativity

Cinnamon

Hazelnut

Pineapple

Pomegranate

✣ Divination

Anise

Bay Leaf

Chamomile

Cherry

Cinnamon

Coffee

Hazelnut

Hibiscus

Jasmine

Juniper

Lavender

Peppermint

Pomegranate

Rose

Saffron

Strawberry

Thyme

⇢ Energy

Cinnamon

Coffee

Vanilla

⇢ Fairies

Elder

Poppy

Violet

⇢ Fertility

Apple

Cherry

Milk

Papaya

Parsley

Peach

Pineapple

Pomegranate

Poppy

⇢ Focus

Sage

Spearmint

⇢ Gaining Favor

Apricot

Maple

Peach

⇢ Happiness

Cherry

Cocoa

Grapefruit

Orange

Peach

Pineapple

Raspberry

Saffron

⇢ Harmony

Lemon

Strawberry

Vanilla

Violet

⇢ Healing

Apple

Almond

Bay Leaf

Blackberry

Chamomile

Cinnamon

Cucumber

Elder

Eucalyptus

Ginger

Lavender

Lime

Nutmeg

Onion

Peppermint

Pineapple

Pumpkin

Nettle

Rose

Rosemary

Saffron

Spearmint

Thyme

Violet

Walnut

→ Immortality/Longevity

Apple

Juniper

Maple

Orange

Peach

Sage

Thyme

→ Love

Agave

Apple

Apricot

Basil

Cardamom

Chamomile

Cherry

Cinnamon

Clove

Cocoa

Cranberry

Ginger

Hibiscus

Jasmine

Lavender

Lime

Maple

Milk

Orange

Papaya

Peach

Pineapple

Poppy

Raspberry

Rose

Saffron

Spearmint

Strawberry

Sugarcane

Thyme

Tomato

Vanilla

Violet

→ Luck

Chamomile

Cherry

Cinnamon

Lemon

Pomegranate

Nutmeg

Rose

Strawberry

Violet

→ Lust

Agave

Cardamom

Chili Pepper

Cinnamon

Cranberry

Ginger

Hibiscus

Nettle

Parsley

Saffron

Vanilla

Violet

→ Mental Clarity

Basil

Bergamot

Coffee

Grapefruit

Lavender

Rosemary

Vanilla

Walnut

→ Money/Prosperity

Almond

Bergamot

Blackberry

Blueberry

Chamomile

Cocoa

Elder

Ginger

Jasmine

Maple

Nutmeg

Peppermint

Pineapple

Pomegranate

Pumpkin

Vanilla

→ Power

Cinnamon

Ginger

Rosemary (*mental power*)

→ Protection

Anise

Basil

Bay Leaf

Blackberry

Blueberry

Cinnamon

Cranberry

Chrysanthemum

Eucalyptus

Hazelnut

Juniper

Lavender

Lime

Nettle

Onion

Parsley

Pineapple

Rose

Rosemary

Sage

Sugarcane

Tomato

Violet

→ Purification

Anise

Bay Leaf

Chamomile

Grapefruit

Lavender

Lemon

Parsley

Peach (*purification through the manifestation of love*)

Peppermint

Sage

Sugarcane

Thyme

Turmeric

→ Reversing

Nettle

→ Sleep

Chamomile

Elder

Jasmine

Lavender

Peppermint

Rosemary

Thyme

Violet

→ Spirit Connection

Anise

Cinnamon

Chrysanthemum

Jasmine

Lavender

Milk

Sage

✢ Strength

Bay Leaf

Ginger

Saffron

Thyme (*courage*)

✢ Success

Almond

Bay Leaf

Cinnamon

Saffron

✢ Wisdom

Almond

Apple

Basil

Bay Leaf

Hazelnut

Sage

Walnut

✢ Youth

Agave

Anise

Cucumber

Peach

Bibliography

Bobrow, Warren. *Bitters & Shrub Syrup Cocktails: Restorative Vintage Cocktails, Mocktails & Elixirs.* Fair Winds Press, 2015.

Cunningham, Scott. *The Complete Book of Incense, Oils & Brews.* Llewellyn Publications, 2002.

Cunningham, Scott. *Cunningham's Encyclopedia of Magical Herbs.* Llewellyn Publications, 1985.

Cunningham, Scott. *Cunningham's Encyclopedia of Wicca in the Kitchen.* Llewellyn Publications, 2002.

Gately, Iain. *Drink: A Cultural History of Alcohol.* Gotham Books, 2008.

Kynes, Sandra. *Llewellyn's Complete Book of Correspondences: A Comprehensive & Cross-Referenced Resource for Pagans & Wiccans.* Llewellyn Publications, 2013.

Kynes, Sandra. *Plant Magic: A Year of Green Wisdom for Pagans & Wiccans.* Llewellyn Publications, 2017.

Mankey, Jason. *Witch's Wheel of the Year: Rituals for Circles, Solitaries & Covens.* Llewellyn Publications, 2019.

McCarthy, Juliana. *The Stars Within You: A Modern Guide to Astrology.* Roost Books, 2018.

Millett, Deacon. *Hoodoo Honey and Sugar Spells: Sweet Love Magic in the Conjure Tradition*. Lucky Mojo Curio Company, 2013.

Morrison, Dorothy. *The Craft: A Witch's Book of Shadows*. Llewellyn Publications, 2001.

Morrison, Dorothy. *Everyday Moon Magic: Spells & Rituals for Abundant Living*. Llewellyn Publications, 2004.

Morrison, Dorothy. *Everyday Sun Magic: Spells & Rituals for Radiant Living*. Llewellyn Publications, 2005.

Regan, Gary. *The Bartender's Bible: 1001 Mixed Drinks and Everything You Need to Know to Set Up Your Bar*. HarperCollins, 1993.

Simmons, Robert, et al. *The Book of Stones: Who They Are & What They Teach*. North Atlantic Books, 2015.

Yronwode, Catherine. *Hoodoo Herb and Root Magic: A Materia Magica of African-American Conjure & Traditional Formulary Giving the Spiritual Uses of Natural Herbs, Roots, Minerals, and Zoological Curios*. Lucky Mojo Curio Company, 2002.

US/Metric Conversion Chart

VOLUME CONVERSIONS	
US Volume Measure	**Metric Equivalent**
⅛ teaspoon	0.5 milliliter
¼ teaspoon	1 milliliter
½ teaspoon	2 milliliters
1 teaspoon	5 milliliters
½ tablespoon	7 milliliters
1 tablespoon (3 teaspoons)	15 milliliters
2 tablespoons (1 fluid ounce)	30 milliliters
¼ cup (4 tablespoons)	60 milliliters
⅓ cup	90 milliliters
½ cup (4 fluid ounces)	125 milliliters
⅔ cup	160 milliliters
¾ cup (6 fluid ounces)	180 milliliters
1 cup (16 tablespoons)	250 milliliters
1 pint (2 cups)	500 milliliters
1 quart (4 cups)	1 liter (about)

WEIGHT CONVERSIONS	
US Weight Measure	**Metric Equivalent**
½ ounce	15 grams
1 ounce	30 grams
2 ounces	60 grams
3 ounces	85 grams
¼ pound (4 ounces)	115 grams
½ pound (8 ounces)	225 grams
¾ pound (12 ounces)	340 grams
1 pound (16 ounces)	454 grams

Index

Note: Page number in *italics* indicate recipes. Page numbers in **bold** indicate enchanted potentials of alcohols. Page numbers in parentheses indicate noncontiguous references.

T

About the Author

Julia Halina Hadas is a practicing witch, bartender, and avid craft cocktail fanatic. Having worked at a distillery and as a craft cocktail bartender in the San Francisco Bay Area, she combined her love of the craft cocktail movement with her witchcraft practice. She holds a BA in anthropology and is a certified crystal healer, shamanic healer, and Reiki practitioner. You can learn more at her blog, WitchCraftCocktails.com, or on her website, FireLotusCreations.com.